Praise for Lynne Brennan

Whatever else changes in organisations, the ability to develop and sustain individual business relationships across all stakeholder groups will remain as important as ever. Whether leading groups or working one to one, Lynne Brennan has, for over ten years now, helped many of us to maximise the individual contribution that we make as 'ambassadors' for the company.

Robert Parker, Corporate Affairs Manager,
McDonald's Restaurants Ltd.

Before Lynne's intervention our 'one organisation' was nothing of the sort; it was really two separate businesses with totally different histories, values and cultures. . . . Lynne took many of the key principles of her approach and together we turned things around. We communicated like never before: downwards, sideways, upwards and sometimes in directions we didn't know existed . . . the board worked exceptionally hard at getting out and talking to everyone in the organisation, not through e-mails or corporate memos, but by encouraging straight talking and constructive criticism. . . . Every employee had the opportunity to say where and how we could improve. . . . Lynne's really special skill is working both one to one and in teams to help those who make an organisation click to adjust their behaviours and embody the vision and change they seek.

Paul Rose, former Human Resources Manager,
Cable & Wireless, Ireland.

I have worked with Lynne in three businesses now; all have been in the technology sector and have varied in size and international presence. On all occasions I have been impressed by Lynne's attitude, professionalism and quite remarkable ability to relate to business people at all levels both in the UK and overseas. Consequently, it is excellent news to see a totally revised edition of her *The Complete Book of Business Etiquette*. Once again, the book sets out readily applicable insights and observations on doing business both ethically and effectively. I am quite sure it will prove extremely valuable to a wide range of people in organisations of all sizes and sectors.

Will Duncan, former Vice President, Human Resources, MSI Ltd.

Lynne has coached a number of people for whom I've had responsibility, with outstanding results. From a personal perspective, Lynne has assisted me in learning how to deal with a huge variety of different situations and people. . . . Lynne has shown me how to remove personal emotion from situations, not to take things personally, really listen to people and develop relationships. In addition, she has provided me with guidance as to how to use limited resources to manage a large workload through improved communication and planning sessions.

Lianne Lambert, Human Resources Manager,
United Management Technologies.

Business Etiquette

for the 21st Century

What to do – and what NOT to do

Lynne Brennan

PIATKUS

Dedication

For Orla and Bump, two very precious souls.

Copyright © 2003 by Lynne Brennan

First published in 2003 by
Judy Piatkus (Publishers) Limited
5 Windmill Street
London W1T 2JA
e-mail: info@piatkus.co.uk

The moral right of the author has been asserted

A catalogue record for this book is available from the British Library

ISBN 0 7499 2330 X

This book has been printed on paper manufactured with respect for the environment using wood from managed sustainable resources

Editing by Krystyna Mayer and Jan Cutler
Text design by Paul Saunders

Typeset by Phoenix Photosetting, Chatham, Kent
Printed and bound in Denmark by
Nørhaven A/S, Viborg

Contents

Acknowledgements

To the very best 'right arm and left leg' in the world, Suzy Hughes. So many thanks for all your hard work and support and for always being there for me.

To David Block for his hard work and professionalism, sincerest thanks. Special thanks and acknowledgment to David for writing Chapter 19, on foreign business etiquette.

For love, help and encouragement, my love and thanks to Sarah and Russell, Karen, Nicola and Rachel, Mum and Dad, and my dear sis Carol. For great encouragement and a loving friendship, dearest Annie, a big hug, love and thanks a million.

To Lianne Lambert and Katy Sivyer, my grateful thanks for your contributions to the research; to Carole Harding Roots of Executive Presentations, thanks and love for happy times and help on many projects, particularly 'Taking Responsibility', and for her input on the list on page 31.

My thanks to the press and commercial attachés in the UK-based foreign embassies and consulates and chambers of commerce who checked and verified the information on their countries in Chapter 19, Foreign Business Etiquette.

To all the people I have worked with over the years, my thanks for all you have taught me.

To everyone at Piatkus, thank you, and particularly to Krystyna Mayer, Gill Bailey and Jan Cutler for great support and the very best kind of encouragement anyone could wish for.

To Kevin for being you and for never failing to believe in me. All my love and thanks.

Lynne Brennan

Introduction

First of all, I would like to define what I mean by business etiquette (BE), the subject of this book. BE is an all-encompassing terminology for successful personal skills and communication in the workplace, covering every area of communication, across all disciplines and all eventualities.

Good personal skills will get you noticed. If you have them, you can work with anyone. I believe everyone needs to build better business relationships in order to be recognised as a high performer and to feel a greater sense of achievement. How often do we find ourselves in a situation where, because we don't get on with a particular person or we don't express ourselves properly, we are unable to build a relationship and therefore miss out on an opportunity? We then feel dispirited or blame someone else for our inability to achieve.

You may be just starting out in business, a well-heeled professional, a senior manager in a large corporation or an entrepreneur – whoever you are, wherever you are, *Business Etiquette in the 21st Century* will help you to improve your personal skills and achieve professional success.

In business today we all need to be aware of how to communicate effectively, and that's where having BE skills will give you the leading edge. A company, whether large or small, always has a business plan – even if it is written on the back of an envelope. However, how many companies do you know of that have a communication plan built around achieving their business plan? How many managers wonder why objectives aren't achieved when they believe people know and understand what needs to be done?

BE is about what needs to be done, by whom and when, in a manner that is realistic, respectful and responsible. It is not about p's and q's and prescriptive rules. In the same way that a company needs to communicate effectively, so does each person who makes up that company. People often blame 'the company' for poor communication, yet if you work for a company you are a part of it. Each person therefore has to take responsibility for being a good communicator so that the whole company will be able to communicate efficiently.

You may be the best technician and do a good job, but if you are unable to communicate well, you will be perceived as a person who 'just hasn't got what it takes'. Think of the people you admire most. You'll find that they are not only great at their jobs, but are also able to put others at ease, face up to difficult situations and let people know how they feel without demotivating an individual, a team or a workforce. *Business Etiquette in the 21st Century* shows you how you can emulate their success and be the best you can be.

The advice in this book encourages you to be yourself. In order to achieve real success, you have to be able to adapt in an ever-changing world, act with confidence in new situations and recognise your own strengths and weaknesses. How can you do this if you are trying to be someone whom you are not?

So often in business we admire a trait in another person and try to act as they have done, and then wonder why things go wrong for us. It is so much better to know ourselves and to take responsibility for everything we do and say. Then we really do feel good and are able to achieve success that is recognised by others as a true strength.

▶ Who will Benefit from this Book?

If you are just starting out in your working life, *Business Etiquette for the 21st Century* will act as a valuable reference book – it's a good read from start to finish. If you are already on the career ladder and a manager, there are tips and techniques that will help you to add to, fine tune and enhance your people skills; this is also a good book to dip in and out of when you feel stuck. If you are a senior manager, the book will act as a refresher and give you plenty of new ideas for developing communication in your organisation.

Although most of the advice in the book is relevant wherever in the world you happen to be working, some additional tips for specific countries and regions are covered in a special section on foreign business etiquette.

▶ How the Book Works

I begin with a quick dash through a working day, highlighting some of the little things, which, if thought about and addressed in a positive manner – without ignoring others and thinking only of our own agenda – can make working life a much more pleasant experience.

I then move on to communication between individuals in the workplace (Chapter 2) and provide a communication analysis for introducing BE into your organisation and your business life (Chapter 3). Using straightforward and uncomplicated techniques, you will be able to identify areas you need to work on in order to become an effective communicator and achieve real success in the workplace.

Whether you are just starting out in business or have been working for many years, you need always to be aware of how to look good so that you will achieve a positive impact. Chapter 4 discusses dressing appropriately for your chosen workplace.

Whenever someone attends an interview of any kind, whether for a new job or at review time, both the interviewer and interviewee need to be aware of how to get the best out of the situation, and this is dealt with in Chapter 5. And what about that first day of a new job or project? How many of us have wished for a helping hand to ensure that we inspire management and have that easy level of confidence that makes us, and others, feel comfortable? Chapter 6 gives you that guidance.

Other everyday working-life topics that are covered include letter writing, telephone skills and dealing with the infamous e-mails that seem to inundate our daily lives (Chapter 7), making meetings productive (Chapter 8) and dealing with the occasional 'difficult' person who inevitably crosses our path in the course of our working life (Chapter 9).

How to complain – as well as being able to handle complaints – and working with uncomfortable situations are discussed in Chapters 10 to 13. The social side of business is important and can be very rewarding for both customers and those hosting social events, as long as a few guidelines are adhered to. Chapters 14 to 18 guide you through exhibitions and conferences, hosting and guesting, and corporate events. Finally, there is a section giving hints and tips for those of you who need a quick reference before flying off to do business overseas.

▶ The Background to the Book

In 1991, *The Complete Book of Business Etiquette* was published. I used this as a marketing platform to launch my company, Business Etiquette International. Since then I have coached people at all levels, from student to chief executive, developed and run workshops, and facilitated team and group sessions in Europe, North America and Canada.

I have enjoyed working with large organisations such as BP, British Gas, Cable & Wireless, McDonald's Restaurants and

Marconi, as well as with start-up and medium-sized companies, and in the education and public sector. Each organisation I have worked with has its own distinct culture, processes and means of communicating. Each one recognised the need to improve its communication and knew that the only way to achieve this effectively was by developing its people's personal skills.

As a result of working with so many people at all levels and from many different disciplines, I have no hesitation in saying that good BE will enable you to move forward with confidence, achieve polish in an already successful career and perhaps even give the most senior of managers guidance on the odd occasion.

Chapter 19 deals with business etiquette abroad. David Block has worked closely with foreign embassies, consulates and chambers of commerce to provide an 'at-a-glance' reminder of how cultures and customs vary around the world.

I hope you enjoy using *Business Etiquette for the 21st Century*, that it helps you to become 100 per cent effective, and provides a boost to your career – whatever stage this is at.

Lynne Brennan, October 2002

CHAPTER 1

A Day in the Life of a Working Person

It's the little things that people don't pay much attention to in a working day – the things that irritate, get blown out of proportion or are simply forgotten – that can make your working life very unpleasant on occasions. So let's just consider a number of situations you need to be able to handle in order to help make a working day as stress-free as possible for yourself and those around you.

Wherever you work, in whatever sector, here are some helpful hints and tips for a variety of common situations.

▶ Before Arriving at Work

The working day begins when you get up in the morning; make sure you have had enough sleep so that you can get up in good time to prepare yourself for your day.

Allowing Plenty of Time

If you need to be at work by a certain time, *always* allow plenty of time. You should never catch a bus, train or aircraft, or leave the house, with just enough time to spare. Always allow an additional half an hour: it is so much better to be early. If you are late, people notice and you are considered unreliable and rude.

Keeping People Waiting

It's easy to think, 'OK, I'll just have a few more minutes in bed' and not consider the person who is collecting you or meeting you. There will be occasions when being late cannot be avoided, but make them the exception rather than the rule.

Too Personal to Mention

Can I just say … deodorant – don't forget to use it. If you know you perspire profusely, then have a change of shirt or top ready to change into at lunchtime. There is no excuse for stale perspiration smells wafting through the air. Be sure you are not the person who is kept at a distance by colleagues and clients.

Using a Handkerchief/Tissues

Don't be the person who sniffs their way to work or throughout the day, especially at meetings. It's irritating to others and spoils what is otherwise a smart impression. A handkerchief or a packet of tissues is a must – don't leave home without one.

Travelling to Work

Whether you are driving all the way to work or to the railway or underground station and then travelling on public transport, there are several situations where thought and etiquette are essential.

Parking Considerately

For most of us, parking in a car park is an everyday occurrence, either on our way to work or when we finally arrive at our workplace destination. So often we are rushing and then we reverse into a parking slot without too much care as to where our car is positioned. We then turn around as we walk away and notice that we've parked across the line. Maybe we just think, 'Oh, I'm in too much of a rush to go back and straighten that up!' How inconsiderate is that? And while I am talking about consideration when parking, *never* park in a disabled bay unless you are authorised to do so.

For those of you who have meetings with clients at their premises, remember to leave enough time to park. If you arrive ten minutes before your meeting is due to begin, the chances are that your clients will not be watching out of their window. If, however, you don't leave enough time and the people you are about to meet are waiting for you and see you as you swing into their car park with your radio blaring, you are not creating a good first impression and your meeting will already be off to a bad start.

Working and Talking on Public Transport

It isn't smart to work with confidential documents on public transport. People can read information quite easily if they are sitting next to or opposite you. If you must use commuting time to read briefs or meeting notes, or to mark papers or fill in forms, be discrete and cover up subject headings, names and letterheads. Always write in pencil; fellow passengers cannot read pencil as easily as pen. Oh, and don't discuss your company business or a colleague you are having problems with in a loud voice. Who knows, someone sitting near you may be doing business with your company and the information you are providing will not project a professional image.

To Sit or Not to Sit

In working life, men and women are supposed to be given equal opportunities. However, equal opportunity doesn't mean not considering others. On public transport, whether you are male or female, it shows concern and good manners to offer a seat to a pregnant woman, an older person or anyone who is obviously in pain or discomfort.

Catching an Aircraft

More and more of us seem to use aircraft in order to reach a destination in time to do a day's business. When the flight attendant does their safety briefing, it is essential to listen every time. Yes, *every* time. I seem to live on aircraft these days, and often wonder how many of those people with their heads stuck in newspapers or chatting while the demonstration takes place would be quite so dismissive if an emergency arose. Apart from your own safety, it is simply rude and arrogant to ignore the person who is speaking.

Many people use very long flights to prepare for global meetings. Out come the laptops, and big discussions between colleagues take place as to how they will handle their overseas client meeting. I am not saying people are shouting, but they are none too quiet, and you never know who is listening; people from your client's company may be sitting nearby. It is poor business etiquette (BE) not to consider the implications of discussing business of a confidential nature in a public place.

Using Mobile Telephones

Mobile phones are such an essential part of our working and social lives. But when travelling on public transport or in a shop, discretion is vital. It is irritating to everyone around to hear either an intimate conversation or a large business deal being discussed. Much better to answer a caller with, 'It's difficult for me to speak right now – I'll call you back in 20 minutes' or, 'I'm on a train/bus/in a shop at the moment; I'll give you a call as soon as possible.'

▶After You Arrive at Work

A pleasant and friendly manner and consideration for others at the workplace will mean that you will benefit from their positive reactions in return.

Opening Doors

It doesn't matter whether we are male or female, young or old, we should all open doors for one another. And certainly don't be the one who is in such a rush that you let a door swing back into the face of the person following you.

Greeting Colleagues

The first greeting of the day with colleagues or customers gives an important first impression. How often have you been the recipient of a grunt and been put off going any further with a conversation? You'll certainly remember situations like that for all the wrong reasons. A bright and sincere greeting for anyone you meet whenever you arrive at work shows warmth of character and makes others feel good. Notice how the atmosphere improves when everyone greets one another properly.

'Did You Have a Good Evening/Weekend?'

Social chat with colleagues is an essential part of building camaraderie and team spirit – but be aware of how much chit-chat you take part in. When someone asks you if you've had a good evening or weekend, you really shouldn't give them chapter and verse of your every movement. It's different if you are in a pub or wine bar after work – then more detail is great – but in the workplace keep it short and simple: 'It was great, thanks' and, if need be, 'I'll tell you more at lunchtime/this evening.'

▶ During the Working Day

Thinking BE while you are at work makes for a smoother day for you and your colleagues.

Eating in

Sandwiches and coffee are an accepted part of working life. Although we know we should take a break at lunchtime to clear our head and refresh ourselves, many of us eat in more often than not. The problem comes when people bring in food such as fish and chips, or Chinese or Indian takeaways. These might be delicious at home – and in the office too – but your colleagues and customers will have to suffer an unpleasant whiff all afternoon. Not very professional and unnecessary when you consider the wide variety of sandwiches available. If you must eat hot food, eat it out of the workplace.

When You Ask a Question

Always ensure that you are listening and showing interest in a person's answer when you have asked them a question. How often in your working day do you experience a person asking a question and being in too much of a rush to hear the answer? It's very frustrating when this happens, and it is also a waste of time as nobody achieves anything.

Giving Compliments

No one really enjoys remarks about dress, hair or achievement when they are gushing and over-exuberant. But sincere acknowledgements, quietly given, mean a great deal to most people. It also feels good to make someone smile. Give and take: it's simple but very effective. And if you are complimented, enjoy the moment; don't feel embarrassed and think you have to say something smart in response. A simple thank you and a warm smile are all that is required.

Avoiding Vulgarity

Why do people believe that telling tasteless and crude jokes will make them popular? I remember a very embarrassing occasion when I was the new girl at a company; to welcome me a group of people asked me to join them for lunch. One man saw it as an occasion to test my sense of humour with a really obscene tale. He laughed at the end – but *no one* else did. Being crude and telling tasteless jokes can make you the butt of a joke, so tell tales of this ilk at your peril! Bad manners and rudeness are signs of insecurity and an inability to accept situations you are not used to. A good rule of thumb for these occasions is, 'If in doubt, say nowt!'

Talking About Rather than Talking to

There will be occasions when a colleague upsets you. If you do not address the situation at the time, it will fester inside you – and you may end up making a mountain out of a molehill. Or maybe you will cause a bad atmosphere by talking to everyone but the person who has upset you. It is so much better to ask the colleague quietly if you can speak to them privately (over a cup of coffee often works wonders).

Start your conversation by saying, 'This is difficult for me, but I need to tell you that I feel really upset about what you said about me the other day. I'd like to talk it through with you, as I feel miserable about it and know it is affecting the atmosphere between us.' Then listen and if the colleague gets angry don't overreact. Keep calm, talk the problem through and make sure you really clear the air. Leave after your coffee, both feeling OK, and be prepared to let bygones be bygones.

This simple technique works: it makes you feel better because you have said how you feel about a situation in a calm and assertive manner. The other person doesn't feel awkward or threatened because you have handled the matter in a considerate way.

Being Overly Familiar

It is one thing being friendly, but when you cross the boundary and become overly familiar, familiarity can begin to breed contempt. Being friendly with colleagues is great, but don't ask personal questions. Let them give you the clue about what they feel comfortable talking about. Some people prefer not to discuss their private lives and that should be respected. Oh, and by the way, if you happen to be a telesales person telephoning private homes in the evening, do address people as 'Sir' or 'Madam' and not by their first names when you begin a conversation. Too much familiarity upsets many people and it won't help your sales quota.

Laughing With and Laughing At

Laughter is a wonderful tonic, and the greater the team spirit in a company, the more people feel relaxed and able to share a joke or pull one another's leg, and that really is wonderful – that is until the leg-pulling goes too far and suddenly you are laughing at someone in a demeaning and, on occasions, nasty way. There is nothing worse than seeing a group of people laughing raucously and an individual trying hard to laugh but failing because they feel demeaned. So laugh with, but laugh at, at your own expense only. Laughing at others is a bully tactic and shows an aggressive attitude and a lack of self-esteem.

Holding Three Meetings in One

Many of you will spend hours at meetings – well chaired or otherwise. One of the rudest things anyone can do is to initiate an on-the-side conversation or mutter to a neighbour in an inaudible tone. Meetings take so much longer because of the additional meetings that take place while the main one is being conducted. Please do not be the initiator of secondary discussions.

Talking to the Boss

'The boss' should never be a hallowed figure. Bosses are human beings, so talking to them should be relaxed and purposeful. Many people find talking to senior people difficult. Don't get hung up on titles. Talk to the person.

Don't ever go to a boss with a problem that you haven't thought through. I remember working for a sales director who had a really effective way of making people do just that. Placed on his desk was a card turned to face the door. On it was written: 'What is your problem and what is your solution?' Many's the time you would get as far as the door and then turn back realising you hadn't given an issue enough thought. So always go to your boss with a solution and the actions to overcome a problem.

Making Personal Calls

There goes that telephone again. No, it isn't a business call; it is yet another personal call. Of course we all have personal calls, but keeping them to a minimum avoids upsetting colleagues and getting you a reputation for being good at socialising but not at your job.

Whose Responsibility is it?

There are many times in a working day when situations occur that aren't necessarily part of our job description. You go to the loo and the loo roll needs replacing; you finish photocopying and know more paper is needed; someone has left their desk and forgotten to put their voicemail on – their phone is ringing and nobody is answering it. What should you do? Use your initiative; don't just expect somebody else to do it. You do it. Everyone appreciates consideration, don't they?

Too Busy to Serve

Nothing irritates me more than walking into a shop and being greeted by two assistants discussing their latest date, while I am standing like a dummy waiting to be served – and when I say, 'Excuse me, could I pay for this please?' I am looked at as if I am being very unreasonable because I've interrupted the conversation. Have any of you experienced this type of situation? If you work in a shop, your greeting is a vital ingredient in customer service and in ensuring that the customer returns to buy more. A smile and acknowledgement cost nothing, but they achieve so much.

▶ Leaving Work

There are people who walk around with a piece of paper in their hand, talking to others all day long. They appear at every single meeting without knowing why they are there, and begin work, saying, 'I am just *so* busy,' just when everyone else is leaving to go home. Such people are not efficient high-flyers. Yes, there will be times when we need to work long hours, but it shouldn't be the norm. People who work late every night are caught on the hamster wheel. Stop. Take a look at how effective you are in the day and make a deal with yourself to leave on time at least twice a week. Practise being the one who says goodnight to colleagues first.

That's just one day and a good one at that. And the underlying need in each situation was for good BE *communication* ...

CHAPTER 2

Silent and Spoken Communication

Dr Albert Mehrabian, Professor Emeritus of Psychology at the University of California since 1994, in his book *Silent Messages* said that three v's – visual, vocal and verbal – make up the communication signals we send to others. Our overall presence is made up by the following three v's:

Visual	How you look	55%
Vocal	How you sound	38%
Verbal	What you say	7%

It's amazing, isn't it, that so many of us spend so much time concentrating on what we actually say without giving too much thought about how we say it. The essence of business etiquette (BE) is to concentrate not only on the content, but also on the delivery. It is necessary to perfect your job skills, but what is the point of being brilliant technically if you are unable to present yourself in a manner that encourages others to speak and listen to you?

Chapter 4 deals with part of the first v: visual, a mighty 55 per cent of our credibility factor. The visual percentage also includes our silent messages: body language, facial expressions and the all-important eye contact, all of which are discussed here, as is the essential skill of listening.

▶ Understanding Body Language

People respond to body language. It is therefore important to know your body-language habits. For example, I know that if I am uncomfortable in a situation, I immediately begin twisting my wedding ring around. The reason I do this is because my wedding ring represents the person who gave it to me, whom I trust and rely on and who gives me support and comfort when he knows I'm feeling unsure. That's great for me. But if I am speaking to a group of people and start fiddling with my ring, initially they may think, 'Oh, she's nervous' and not take too much notice. However, if I continue to fiddle: (a) they won't listen to what I'm saying because my fiddling will disturb their concentration, (b) they will probably begin to feel quite irritated, and (c) my credibility will have flown out of the window because how can someone who is supposed to be an expert on a subject appear so nervous for so long?

Body language isn't always just one movement. Very often it is more than one, but you can be assured that if your non-verbal signals are out of kilter with your spoken message, the people listening to you will feel uncomfortable, or may not believe – or be interested in – what you are saying.

Body language is such an important part of any spoken inter-action that it really is worth continually observing and developing your ability to read others' signals. Try turning down the volume on a television programme and watching the gestures people use to express themselves. People-watching is a favourite pastime of mine and I would encourage you to use time in airports, railway stations and restaurants, and at business or social gatherings, to observe people's emotions and gestures. As well as making you more aware of your own body language, habits and gestures, your observance of others will boost your ability to communicate more effectively.

Here is a list of some observed body-language habits. What do they mean to you?

1. Running fingers through the hair.

2. Sitting back with both hands behind the head.

3. Legs crossed, arms tightly folded.

4. Sitting forward, head nodding occasionally.

5. Supporting the head in the right hand with an elbow resting on a table.

6. Foot tapping, fist clenched.

7. Hands over eyes.

8. Direct, strong eye contact.

9. Stroking the chin.

10. Hair-twisting.

11. Rubbing an earlobe.

12. Tight-lipped with both hands on hips.

Here is a list of my interpretations – see if yours are the same:

1. Unsure/frustrated or angry.
2. Know it all.
3. Defensive/annoyed.
4. Interested.
5. Bored/tired.
6. Frustrated/angry.
7. Does not want to see someone/something; disappointed/ frustrated/angry.
8. Aggressive/dominant.

9. Deep in thought.
10. Nervous.
11. Nervous/doubtful/not telling the truth.
12. Aggressive.

Interesting, isn't it? We don't realise how much we are saying to people without opening our mouths, do we?

Just a tip: ask someone who knows you really well to tell you what your irritating body-language habits are, and don't ignore what they say. If it irritates them, you can be sure it is irritating a colleague or a customer ... or both.

▶ Making Eye Contact

Good eye contact is essential to build trust, to encourage others and to be credible. It does not mean staring directly at someone's face, or holding another's eyes with an unflinching gaze, which can appear cold and intimidating.

Good eye contact does mean looking at a person's face and moving your eyes from theirs to other parts of their face.

The following three gazes indicate the importance of not staring someone out or letting your eyes wander.

Professional Gaze

Look at the eyes and at a point in the middle of the forehead (this is often referred to as the third eye).

This gaze is used when you walk into a group situation or room for the first time. For those of you addressing large groups of people and having to make presentations, this gaze allows you to look around a room full of people without becoming transfixed on one particular person. It also enables you to build empathy with your audience and make each person feel you are speaking to them.

Social Gaze

Look at the eyes and around the face, taking in the nose and mouth.

This gaze can be used in any situation but is particularly effective when communicating on a one-to-one basis. Your eyes don't have to come out on stalks and be continually scanning a person's face, but looking at a person's nose or mouth when speaking to them softens the eye contact and puts people at ease.

Personal Gaze

The personal gaze is a no-go gaze in business. The minute the gaze moves below the chin, it makes the person to whom you are speaking feel uncomfortable.

This gaze is definitely for personal relationships only. Even if you just look at a person's shoes and then back to their face, it makes them feel that you are looking them up and down.

If you are subjected to the rudeness of a person looking at any part of your anatomy below your chin, place your hand just below your chin on the upper chest region and then move your hand slightly upwards and to the side as a gesture. You will have given a clear signal that the offender's eyes should be focused on your face and their eyes will follow your hand; be sure to bring your hand back to a suitable spot – the chin maybe.

▶ Reading Facial Expressions

You have probably heard someone say, 'The trouble with me is that I can't hide what I am feeling – I know it always shows on my face.' Fact: we all show what we think or feel in our facial expressions. Even if we believe we can cover up our true feelings, we don't. However brief the expression – a secondary flash in the eyes, a lifting of an eyebrow or a pursing of the lips – in that moment we have shown anger, surprise or frustration.

In the same way as we use gestures, our face also emphasises how we feel; the problem comes when our facial expression is at odds with what we are articulating verbally.

Just consider these expressions:

A smiling face A smile is the number-one communication signal the world over. It encourages others, warms people to the message you are giving, gives energy to your voice and makes you feel good. I am not saying you have to walk around looking like a Cheshire cat all the time, because there are occasions when smiling is inappropriate, but as a general rule, a smile lightens both other people's spirits and your own.

A disgruntled face No need to ask how this person feels. Dissatisfied, even angry I would say. If you feel this unhappy with something, your whole being is agitated and disgruntled. The trap we sometimes fall into is believing that if we don't say we are dissatisfied or beginning to feel angry, the other person won't realise they have upset us. Wrong. We give conflicting messages, and that leads to misunderstandings, poor communication and people believing that we say what they want to hear, not what they need to know.

BE is about letting people know how you feel in a manner that is clear and non-threatening. When you feel disgruntled, dissatisfied or angry, say honestly to the other person, 'I am really beginning to feel frustrated . . .' or, 'I am feeling dissatisfied with . . .' or, 'I am now beginning to feel angry.' This ensures that the spoken words correspond with your facial expression.

An indifferent face This is one of the most negative expressions. It shows no enthusiasm or interest. It is an expression most frequently seen in a meeting situation when a discussion is taking place between two people that is of no particular interest to others. So what happens? People switch off, hence the indifferent look. It also happens when you aren't listening properly because you are too busy thinking about what you are going to say next.

These are just three examples of how facial expressions work for and against us. How often have you been walking down a high street and caught sight of yourself in a shop window? I know that when it's happened to me, I've been quite surprised at how severe an expression I have on my face while I'm completely lost in thought. It's worth looking in a mirror and noting your relaxed facial expression. If you don't make the effort to smile when you greet someone, your first impression could result in a misjudgement, as they may perceive you to be miserable, severe or disinterested.

▶ Using Your Voice Effectively

The effective delivery of your message is dependent upon your tone of voice and the rate and volume at which you speak. That's if you want people to listen to you, take you seriously and remember what you've said. Your voice is a vital part of your personality: no two people speak the same, so don't even try to sound like someone else; you will be judged as sounding false.

How you breathe affects your voice. Breathe deeply from the bottom of your lungs – your voice will be full of energy and you will have sufficient breath to complete your sentences. To be most effective when you are speaking, use your voice by varying your range, volume and tone. Pause for emphasis and pronounce the ends of your words so that people will be able to listen easily. BE is not about being the person who is speaking the loudest and the longest. It is about being clear and concise at a level that is appropriate for your surroundings.

Here is a voice checklist that you will find useful to refer to no matter how used you may be to speaking on a one-to-one basis or to larger groups. It can act as a guide to developing a stronger voice or as an *aide-mémoire*.

VOICE CHECKLIST

Do	Don't
Pronounce the ends of your words.	Gabble.
Use the rate at which you speak to give emphasis.	Speak quickly continuously – people stop listening.
Pause to emphasise and draw attention.	Pause for too long – it makes you appear arrogant.
Know how softly you can speak and still gain attention.	Speak loudly and out of context.
Be aware of the correct volume for the number of people you are addressing.	Lower your head when you begin to speak – you will be deemed to be mumbling from the start.
Consider the person (or people) you are speaking to.	Think facts are more important than your tone of voice.
Be enthusiastic, clear and concise.	Drone on in a monotonous tone.

▶Improving Your Listening Skills

For me, listening is one of the all-important skills. I am sure you, like me, can list numerous occasions when you know someone hasn't been listening to you and likewise many occasions when you have been too busy to listen to others. It doesn't matter where you are on the career ladder; good listening skills set you apart, give you credibility and enable you to be more efficient and successful.

Here is a quick test to check how good your listening skills are. Do this very quickly, ticking yes or no next to each of the questions. It shouldn't take you any longer than three minutes.

WHEN LISTENING TO OTHERS ...

	Yes	No
Do you let your mind wander?	☐	☐
Does your body language tell people you are bored or in a hurry to move on?	☐	☐
Do you think about your own ideas?	☐	☐
Do you think about what you will say next?	☐	☐
Are you easily distracted by things going on around you?	☐	☐
Do you pretend to be listening when you are not?	☐	☐
When a person stops speaking, do you jump in immediately with your ideas?	☐	☐
Do you complete the ends of people's sentences?	☐	☐
If you disagree with something that's being said, do you interrupt?	☐	☐
Do you avoid listening to some people?	☐	☐
Do you block out when someone is talking about something which doesn't interest you?	☐	☐
Do you try to stop someone speaking if he or she is getting angry or upset?	☐	☐

The first time I did this, I ticked yes next to most of the questions. We are all very task-oriented, aren't we – needing to achieve objectives, to make sure deadlines are met, to do what we see as our priority without really stopping to think about others.

If you have three or more ticks in the yes column, then it really will be worthwhile developing your listening skills. All this needs is concentration. The improvement in your ability to communicate more effectively can happen overnight. For all of us in the workplace, and socially, being a good listener is a great life skill. For those of you in management, good listeners motivate others and have a positive impact on morale.

LISTENING SKILLS CHECKLIST

Do	Don't
Pay attention to everything that is said and not said.	Let your mind wander – people know when it does!
Be alert to the tone and any changes in the speaker's voice.	Just listen for facts.
Give visual signs that you are listening to what is being said.	Continuously write notes while someone is speaking.
Ask people to say more about anything you don't understand.	Ass-u-me anything (it makes an ass out of u and me). You'll end up not fully appreciating another's message.
Listen carefully when people express doubts or concerns.	Ignore them.

Do	Don't
Be able to repeat what the speaker has said, rephrased in your own words.	Think that because you have nodded continuously or mmm'd enthusiastically you have listened.
Pause before you suggest an idea after a person stops speaking.	Overtalk another person or finish sentences for him or her.
Let someone fully explain a situation to you if they are angry or upset.	Interrupt until they have finished.

Silent and spoken communication skills underpin your ability to communicate well in any situation. But communicating effectively is essential within an organisation as a whole as well as between individuals . . .

CHAPTER 3

Communication within the Workplace

Communication. What an overused word that is! It covers so many areas, some of which we probably wouldn't consider being in the communication category, until we really begin to think about *that* word. For me it covers everything from planning efficiently as an organisation and individual, through to each person taking real responsibility for what they say and how they say it. I believe it is at the heart of everything we do as companies and individuals.

Time and again you will hear people say, 'But it wasn't communicated to us' or, 'The problem with this place is poor communication' or, 'If only management would listen to us' or, 'Nobody told us.' You've probably heard some, if not all, of these statements, and for those of you in management or at a senior level, no doubt you have heard them time and again.

The lack of effective communication is the single, largest issue in the workplace. Yes, all right, I hear you say, we know that but what do we actually do about overcoming the issue and putting it right? My answer: each person has to take responsibility for improving communication within their workplace.

▶Step 1

Directors and managers have to take responsibility by making time in their busy schedules to develop a communication plan that is as meaningful as the company's business plan.

Developing a Communication Plan

Organise facilitated sessions to discover what your people believe needs to be done to improve communication. Identify a person who will be responsible for driving 'The Communication Project'. Your objective is to discover what your workforce believes are the strengths and weaknesses of your company's communication and what three actions they feel need to be taken to build on the strengths and overcome the weaknesses. The facilitator or project leader then collates the material: it usually results in information being categorised under five to six major headings.

In a process such as this there will be repetition, but this highlights those areas that need to be addressed as priorities. It is unreasonable to expect all the suggested actions to be top priorities, but for you as management to agree to the implementation of one action a month really does improve morale and communication in general. Why? Because if something is being done as a result of your workforce's input, they then believe that management is truly listening to them. It is a two-fold benefit process, as you also have a document that forms the basis of a communication plan.

▶Step 2

Everyone in the company, including management at all levels, needs to take responsibility and do a self-assessment. Ask yourself, 'What are my strengths and weaknesses as a communicator?'

and make sure you date the document. A simple layout such as the following is all you need.

ASSESSMENT CHART

Example:

Kevin Michaels   **Date: 03.04.02**

Strengths   **Weaknesses**

Strong written communication skills.

Lack confidence when talking to hierarchy.

Set my objectives for achieving results.

Tend to waffle when giving my opinion at meetings.

Find it easy to talk to people I know.

Can take on too much.

▶ Step 3

Once you have produced your strengths and weaknesses assessment, make your own action list to build on your strengths and overcome your weaknesses.

ACTION LIST

Action   **Date**

Don't get hung-up on titles. Remember to build empathy with people. Recognise that I am talking to a fellow human being rather than a title.

Opportunity to practise at the new product launch in two weeks' time.

Action	Date
Use past, present and future technique to keep my thoughts on track:	Use technique at weekly product meeting on Friday.
Past: when we met last month, this was the situation . . .	
Present: we are currently working on . . .	
Future: by next month, we will have completed x and be working on y.	
Learn to be more assertive so that I can say no without feeling rude or guilty.	Book myself on to assertiveness workshop on 13 May 2002.

Once you have completed your self-assessment and compiled your dated action list, use it to monitor your progress. Most of us have more than three strengths and weaknesses, so don't feel you are unusual if you produce long lists, and certainly don't be concerned if your weaknesses list is longer. The greatest strength is to identify your weaknesses, because then you can do something about overcoming them. You also need to concentrate on utilising your strengths.

▶Step 4

Now you have faced up to knowing yourselves 'warts and all', you are in a better position to build empathy with others. Knowing and admitting to yourself that you are not perfect overcomes tendencies to set unrealistic goals for yourself. It also makes you aware of the areas you need to work on.

▶ Being the Best Communicator You Can Be

If you are to project good personal skills and build better business relationships, which is after all what real success in the workplace means, this is what *you* are responsible for.

▶ Your behaviour and how it affects others.

▶ Your goals and expectations.

▶ Your tendency to blame.

▶ Your vocabulary.

▶ Your attitude to risk-taking.

▶ Your credibility.

▶ Your ability to turn negative into positive.

▶ Your stress levels.

▶ Your choices.

▶ Your relationships with difficult people.

▶ Your approach to career mentors.

▶ Your business relationships.

▶ Your actions after making mistakes.

▶ Your international relationships.

▶ Yourself and your personal fulfilment.

When you look at this list, you will realise that there is no way out. It's up to you.

You develop interpersonal skills effectively through silent, spoken and written communication. Part of silent communication includes how you appear to others. Appearance hinders or quickens your progression in the working world, so it is worth looking carefully at it.

CHAPTER 4

Dressing Appropriately

If you are to make the best possible impression, dressing appropriately for what you do in a working day is essential. Not only does your self-confidence benefit, but it also shows you have given thought to others and the situation. I believe it's always worth remembering the constantly used advertising guideline: 'Perception is 98 per cent reality'. Why? Because you are a product and you are selling yourself every minute of every day, so being well groomed and dressing appropriately for what you do is an important ingredient in making your appearance work for you.

▶ Company Styles

A company usually has its own traditions and levels of fashion. These relate to its field of activity and what has been established by its senior executives. If you are a new recruit and unsure of what to wear, the simple rule is to follow their lead to start with.

For those of you who have a uniform to wear, whether it is for a bank, hospital, hotel, restaurant, shop or office, it is worth remembering that the uniform is only as smart as the person wearing it. It's so easy to take for granted an outfit that has been provided and not look after it in the same way as you would if you had bought it yourself. Pressing, dry-cleaning and washing your uniform regularly will ensure that you always look good and show others you care. Caring is a good attitude to develop. People who care deliver quality results, and that gets you noticed.

You should always present yourself well and be noticed for the right reasons. You never know what is around the corner or who notices and recommends when promotions or new job opportunities arise. Picture yourself in your clothes for work. Does your outfit match your job? Business dress codes vary tremendously from company to company, and if you work in a large organisation, dress code may even vary from department to department. A general tip: if in doubt, err on the smart side – smart conservative, smart casual, smart very casual, or smart trendy.

Here are some general guidelines, but there will always be exceptions to any rule, and my advice is to use your initiative and be guided by the expected and accepted within your particular workplace.

For:		
	Law	Smart conservative.
	Medical	Smart conservative.
	City	Generally smart conservative, but check if your company has a 'dress-down day' and if it does, smart casual is the order of the day.
	Publishing	Smart casual to conservative.
	Computer	Very casual to conservative.
	Consultancy	Smart casual to conservative.
	Music	Casual to trendy to conservative.
	Art/Design	Very casual to trendy to conservative.
	Television	Smart casual to trendy.

▶ Cost

There is a rule that covers every element of the business wardrobe, be it clothing, shoes, accessories or grooming: buy the best you can afford.

You don't have to go to extremes. Between tat and clothes costing hundreds are those obtainable from good department and chain stores. And for the patient, there are the bargains in the sales.

Good-quality clothes are an important investment. They will last a long time when cared for, and will probably be worth altering to stay in tune with fashion, or storing for when the fashion swings back ... and that happens more often than I really care to admit.

▶ Working with a Fashion Consultancy

There are many well-qualified people who specialise in ensuring that you wear the correct clothes and colours to make the most of your skin tone, figure or physique. Business etiquette (BE) doesn't cover such a specialist area; we leave that to the experts. It really is worth the outlay of a consultation with such a person, as their advice can save you money and you can be confident knowing the style is right for you.

A fashion consultant will:

▶ **Tell** you which colours, shapes and designs are best for you.

▶ **Appraise** your character, personality and job, and recommend styles that enhance them.

▶ **Help** you decide not only what looks good on you, but also what you will enjoy wearing.

▶ **Escort** you to unexplored and more flattering sartorial elegance.

Best of all, a consultant won't recommend that you lose weight! Consultants worth their title are too canny for that. You will simply be shown how to 'optimise' your present shape – we like that.

▶ Referring to Magazines

Magazines are an excellent source of new ideas. But there is a pitfall into which many totter by not immediately recognising that photographic models are built differently from us ordinary folk: they are usually much taller, narrower and trimmer. And clothes don't always fit them properly either. Look behind the scenes at fashion photo sessions and you'll see forests of hidden pins and mountains of tape, padding and clamping.

Check what suits you

▶ Stay clear of the latest fashions if they don't actually suit you.

▶ Buy only what *you* look good in and feel comfortable in.

▶ Make sure that your clothes express self-confidence.

▶ Women's Style

Most organisations now allow women to express themselves fairly freely in what they wear. Only a few years ago, women wearing trouser suits were often frowned upon in many situations, but they are now accepted. A suggested working wardrobe could include:

▶ At least one classic suit in a basic colour: plain navy, black or grey.

▶ Classic jackets, skirts and trousers. The more basic the colour, the more you can interchange.

▶ Plain dresses that look good under those jackets.

▶ Accessories that reveal your style and individuality, such as earrings, necklace, scarf or brooch.

▶ Good-quality, long-sleeved shirts/tops (but not strappy ones).

▶ Court shoes in black leather or patent.

▶ A smart coat.

▶ … and have you gone for quality over quantity? If so, you'll look better all round.

There are still some people who require a more formal code of dress, such as those who do business in rigidly traditional countries and specific types of business, for example law.

Wearing black and white, or all black, every day needs additional care when choosing outfits in order to maintain a professional, sharp look. In particular, the cut of a black dress, skirt and jacket has to be right for you. Lightening up black with a black and white scarf, or a crisp white shirt or top, can't be beaten. Good use of jewellery with black also livens up your appearance. And pieces of costume jewellery or the real stuff can be as small or as large as suits you. Just don't fall into the trap of large and swinging – from the ears or around your neck. It makes people notice your jewels rather than listen to what you say.

▶ Men's Style

In many areas of business today, the traditional suit is replaced by more casual attire. But, as in the case of women's dress, there are specific areas of business where a two-piece suit is still expected. This can appear to be a limiting factor for a man wanting to project his personality and a professional image, but it need not be so if your suit is well cut and navy, charcoal or grey: the power colours.

Shirts worn with suits should always be long-sleeved with a small amount of cuff showing beneath the jacket sleeve. White is always safest for shirts, and some say it's the best choice. Pale blue and striped shirts are also acceptable in most organisations.

Ties should be in solid colours, striped or patterned, and should tone with your shirt but not shout at it. Generally avoid cartoon characters on ties for the workplace; they are great fun, but you do want to be taken seriously. A tip here: if you are making a presentation, make sure your tie veers to the conservative. Loud patterns and colours will certainly get your audience's attention, but it will spend most of its time looking at your tie rather than listening to you. All that hard work and nobody listening to you, just because you didn't think about your choice of tie; a small point, but really significant. Make sure that your tie touches the top of your belt; and by the way, a belt should always be worn with a suit or casual trousers.

The recommended minimum for a man's business wardrobe is three suits (usually dark grey or navy in colour), one of which should be in a 'summer weight'; notice the inverted commas if you are UK-based. As I write this, the month is June and a summer-weight suit would certainly need a warm overcoat on top of it today. Although three suits are a recommended minimum requirement, if you are just starting out on the business ladder and have only enough money for one suit, then buy the best you can afford, change out of it as soon as you can at the end of the working day, always hang it up and ensure that it goes to the dry-cleaners regularly.

One other point on colour: brown suits and shoes are normally a no-no in the business world. Unless you are specifically advised to wear brown by an image consultant and it would be accepted in your workplace, forget it.

GENERAL GROOMING CHECKLIST

Do	Don't
Keep your hair trimmed and clean.	Have flowing locks and falling dandruff.
Wear perfume and aftershave – just enough to smell good.	Splash on copious amounts of perfume or aftershave.
Have clean and well-manicured nails.	Leave the remains of a hobby in your nails – paint, grease or earth is not attractive.
Make sure your shoes are clean and in good repair.	Leave home without cleaning your shoes.
Use your clothes brush to ensure your outfit is pristine.	Wear anything that has a stain, flecks of dust, stray hairs or dandruff adorning it.
Look at yourself in a mirror and check hems, buttons and zips.	Forget the back view.
Wear a smart topcoat.	Wear padded jackets, unless you ski to work.

CHECKLIST FOR WOMEN

Do	Don't
Have your nails polished in a fashionable colour and ensure they are chip free – every day.	Choose lurid colours for the workplace.

Do	Don't
Keep a spare pair of stockings or tights handy.	Leave a laddered pair of stockings or tights on your legs.
Wear trainers to run to work, and change into shoes when you arrive.	Leave them on.
Add jewellery that suits you and the outfit you are wearing.	Opt for the swinging or dangling kind.
Wear smart, appropriate clothes for your working life.	Have thigh-high slits in skirts, bra straps showing and too much flesh exposed at chest or midriff level. Oh, and no pant lines either.

CHECKLIST FOR MEN

Do	Don't
Trim beards, moustaches and excessive nose and ear hair.	Leave the remains of a meal in a moustache or beard and forget to trim your nose and ear growth.
Wear a watch, wedding band and dress ring.	Wear more than two rings, one on each hand.
Wear earrings in your leisure time and if you work in an environment where they are accepted.	Wear them in a traditional office or just to make a statement regardless of how much they cost.
Wear black shoes with a business suit.	Wear brown shoes, suede boots or grey or beige shoes with a business suit.

Do

Ensure your socks cover the space between your trouser bottoms and shoe tops when seated.

Wear navy, dark grey or black socks with business suits.

Don't

Flash white flesh in the space between your trouser bottoms and the tops of your socks.

Wear white socks.

In Summary

The ability to choose clothes that suit you and be well groomed is essential if you are to be your own best asset at all times. Gaining confidence in your appearance will eliminate a concern and improve your body language. If you know you look good and feel good, it shows ... and others feel more at ease in your presence. That's a fact whether you have years of experience or none at all.

▶ A Personal Emergency Kit

Keep your own personal emergency kit tucked away in a drawer for the times when you are called to a meeting you weren't expecting, or when you are hotter than you thought you would be and you don't like the aroma that creates, or when a button has fallen off a jacket or a nail breaks. For any number of mini-catastrophes that can occur, having an emergency kit makes you feel more comfortable, because you know you are always prepared for the unexpected.

Every personal emergency kit should include:

▶ Clothes brush/roller brush

▶ Toothbrush and toothpaste

▶ Nail file

▶ Hairbrush and comb

▶ Deodorant

▶ Breath freshener

▶ Shoe shine

▶ Travel sewing kit

▶ Packet of painkillers

▶ Handkerchief/tissues

For women add:

▶ Spare tights or stockings

▶ Make-up basics

For men add:

▶ Spare shirt

▶ Razor or battery shaver

People tend to underestimate the importance of their outward appearance to their sense of self-confidence in the workplace. Dressing appropriately in a style that suits you can greatly enhance your ability to project a confident demeanour – something that is particularly important when you are going for a job interview.

CHAPTER 5

The Job Interview

Job interviews are highly charged situations. The stakes are high and, regardless of how many interviews you attend or conduct, each one will be different. An interview is a two-way process. The interviewee needs to project a confident and capable manner and show that they are right for the job. The interviewer assesses the interviewee to determine whether or not that person has the right skills for the job and if they will fit into the company. In both cases, preparation, having the right attitude, punctuality, and being able to ask and answer questions well are key ingredients to a successful interview.

▶ The Interviewee

Each interview you attend will be different because the interviewer will have their own personal style. You can rely on our business etiquette (BE) tips, but ultimately, it is your personality that has to shine through. You have to show your ability to project a confident manner, which means being well prepared and believing in yourself.

Before the Interview

Once you have been invited to the interview, confirm your acceptance and begin your preparation. You must be prepared to ask questions based upon what your interviewer has told you beforehand and the research you have done. Most companies now have a website, and you can find out a great deal about organisations from this source; ask the company to send you some of its literature to look through so that you can familiarise yourself with its business.

Providing Information About Yourself

You will either have sent in a CV or filled in an application form. Sometimes you send in a CV and, when you arrive for the interview, you are also expected to fill in an application form before the interview begins, so always take a copy of your CV with you for reference. This may may be obvious, but remember what you've written in a CV, because your interviewer will question you from that information, and it doesn't give a good impression if you have to refer to your CV constantly to answer questions.

Ensure that your CV is kept to a maximum of two pages unless you are applying for a position where you know a large amount of detail is expected. People who are interviewing need to absorb as much about you as quickly as possible. There is an excellent book by Tom Jackson called *The Perfect CV* that covers every type of CV you could ever wish to write. From a BE viewpoint, it is important to be clear and concise and to remember that it is the first impression of you that a possible future employer will have. So layout and the quality of information you give need to be the best you can deliver.

Timing Your Arrival

Make sure that you know where the interview is taking place, where the building is and how long it will take you to get there.

Arrive 10–15 minutes before your interview appointment – but no earlier as people have very busy schedules and the interviewer will have assigned the interview time for a reason. When you have a long journey, it is often difficult to gauge the perfect arrival time, but if you have driven, park elsewhere and wait rather than burst in half-an-hour beforehand. If you arrive at your destination an hour or so ahead of your interview due to the way a train's arrival times are scheduled, go into the station restaurant and have something to drink before making your way to your appointment.

You may find yourself in a situation where you have no alternative but to arrive at a company excessively early. In this case, go into the reception area, and explain to the receptionist that you are extremely early for your appointment and that you do not want to disturb your interviewer at such an early hour.

Most reception staff will be comfortable for you to sit in reception until the time for your appointment. They may contact your interviewer and say, 'Your person for interview has arrived. They know they are extremely early but they are in reception.' Don't be disturbed if the interviewer then tells the receptionist to let you sit down in reception until your appointed time. Whatever happens – don't be late! OK, I'll not be quite so adamant here, as sometimes, particularly if you are using trains or aircraft, you can be delayed.

If, despite every effort, you are delayed, you should telephone as soon as you can to give the interviewer an estimate of your time of arrival. Explain briefly and apologise then and there. If you wait until you arrive to apologise, it will have given the interviewer lots of time to think less of you.

Make sure you allow plenty of time for your interview. If you are going to be tight for time (for example, if you only have your lunch hour for the appointment), let your interviewer know before you arrive so that they can rearrange the appointment if they feel you won't have sufficient time.

Creating a Good First Impression

First impressions are critical. It is a fact that a first judgement will be made within 30 seconds. It is then that your interviewer will be thinking, 'I feel comfortable,' 'I'm not sure' or, 'Oh dear,' so it is essential to be well groomed, have a smile on your face, walk with purpose and have a firm handshake. If you do not project a confident image at this stage, it will definitely get the interview off to a negative start.

Your appearance needs to be given careful consideration. Even if the company has a casual dress policy, unless you are specifically told you can dress informally, you should wear formal business dress to interviews. Avoid splashing on the aftershave or wearing too much perfume, as interviews often take place in small rooms.

Introducing Yourself and Addressing Others

In most organisations today, once introductions have been made, people refer to one another by their first names. But do err on the side of caution here – it is always best not to assume you can immediately call a person by their first name unless you are very familiar with the company culture and know that to use first names from the start will be accepted.

When introducing yourself, it is wrong to use Mr, Mrs, Ms or Miss before your name. They are courtesy titles, hence the reason why you can address someone you are meeting for the first time as Mr, Mrs, Ms or Miss.

I have noticed over the last couple of years that Ms isn't used much at all – it seems to me that if people (hotel reception staff particularly) are unsure of a woman's status, they do tend to use Miss. For women only: if someone interviewing you calls you Miss and you are married or prefer to be called Ms, you can correct the interviewer in a pleasant tone; better still, you might try saying, 'I am married/divorced, but please call me [first name] anyway.' This approach is friendly and makes everyone feel at ease.

Displaying a Confident Attitude

An open, self-assured attitude is the best approach, as is communicating in a natural and positive manner. Avoid arrogance at all costs – the company is not lucky that you have turned up for the interview. The two-way process should give you ample opportunity to ask questions and seek information to ensure that both the position you are being interviewed for and the company are right for you, but do be aware of your tone of voice when you ask questions.

Be sure to establish and maintain good eye contact (*see page 19*) and to look and feel relaxed. If you are being interviewed by two people, which can often be the case, speak to both of them. The person asking the question is representing both parties and you should therefore respond to both.

Be careful also not to perch on the edge of your chair. Sit well back and be alert and attentive. Avoid distracting gestures like swinging or permanently fidgeting legs, rummaging around your face or tossing your head back to free your eyes of flowing locks.

Tips on Dealing with Challenging Moments

▸ The interviewer asks, in a friendly manner, 'Would you like tea or coffee or a glass of water?' and adds, 'Do help yourself to biscuits.' Your answer is probably an eager, 'Yes please' to the liquid refreshment, but even if you are tempted by the biscuits, leave well alone. They can be crumbly (don't even think about dunking!) and you may be caught chewing just as a quick answer is required.

▶ The interviewer smiles and says, 'Tell me about yourself.' Where do you begin and finish? It's one of those statements that can wrongfoot the most experienced and professional person. The purpose of such an enquiry is for the interviewer to gain an appreciation of your personality and to judge whether or not you will fit into their organisation. Use the 'past, present and future technique' below to help you focus on an appropriate reply.

▶ You need to be clear and concise and not ramble on, giving unending details about past experiences, especially if they are totally irrelevant to the job you are applying for. Neither do you want to give vivid accounts of your sporting prowess and list endless hobbies that will leave the interviewer wondering how committed you are to actually working.

Using the Past, Present and Future Technique

I have found that a technique based on past, present and future can be a helpful way to describe your past career and future aspirations in an interview. It has proved to be really useful to people I coach and groups I work with. Although simple it is very effective. Let me give you an example of how you can use it in this context:

Past   'I first realised I wanted to be a software engineer
         when I was in my last year at school. We had an
         excellent tutor who really influenced my thinking. So
         I went to university and gained my degree in
         computer sciences. I then worked for Microsoft and
         am now with Oracle and ...

Present '... am currently working on a consultancy project that
         has enabled me to realise just how much experience I

have gained over the years and also what I really want to specialise in. I saw your advertisement ...

Future '... and believe that I fit the technical requirements you are looking for. I am keen to work with a young team and develop others. I am looking forward to completing my MBA in July when I return from the family holiday; I am also hoping to play some golf and read a number of books that have been recommended to me.'

Using this technique you can keep your thoughts on track and give a professional impression. You have also given information that will enable the interviewer to ask further questions to gain more in-depth knowledge.

However much the interviewer may probe, don't malign your current or former employers. It's a loser's approach and pays cheap and short-term dividends. If you are seen to be disdainful and overly critical, your interviewer may wonder if one day you would subject them to a similar assault.

Some Helpful Hints

▶ **Personal questions** You don't have to give detailed answers to personal questions. In the UK you should not be asked if you are married, divorced, have children, etc., and if you are, give a brief answer and try to move the interview on.

▶ **Objections** If something is said that you disagree with, you should politely say so. Should the interviewer stick on a fundamental issue with which you disagree, you must maintain your integrity – failure to do so is at your future peril – but don't get agitated. Just stay calm and stick to how you feel.

▶ **Self-respect** However badly you need the job, always be true to yourself and never allow anyone to be rude to you.

▶ **Money** You should not broach the subject of money before all details of the job have been covered. In an ideal world, the salary level will be based on your experience, expertise, contribution and anticipated working performance. If it isn't, don't show resentment; be realistic and negotiate or accept the sum being offered.

▶ **The circuit** If you are given a tour around the company, it isn't a free excursion. It's an opportunity for you to sense the atmosphere of the working environment. Get involved by asking questions about the information you are being given.

Making a Dignified Exit

When the interview is clearly at an end, regardless of how you think you got on, smile and thank the interviewer for seeing you. If appropriate, ask when the decision will be made and when you will be informed. Shake hands, say goodbye and leave, without standing around and stuttering in the doorway.

The Follow-up

When you hear the verdict, whether you have been successful or not write a short thank-you note on your own notepaper to the interviewer. It will not be unappreciated and will make you feel good too.

Whether you are about to attend an interview or have already attended one or many, the following dos and don'ts checklist will be a useful reference for you.

CHECKLIST FOR INTERVIEWEES

Do	Don't
Prepare: know something about the company and its marketplace.	Expect to know as much about the company as the person who interviews you.
Be on time.	Be late or excessively early.
Allow plenty of time for the interview.	Arrive and tell the interviewer what time you need to leave.
Be yourself.	Show any degree of arrogance.
Be enthusiastic.	Talk all the time.
Dress appropriately.	Wear casual clothes unless specifically told to do so.
Smile and walk with purpose into the interview room.	Shuffle, walk with your head down or swagger into the room.
Have a firm handshake.	Offer a limp hand or give a knuckle-crushing handshake.
Listen attentively.	Interrupt.
Ask questions relevant to the job.	Ask unnecessary questions and sound as if you are interrogating the interviewer.
Go well prepared and allow time for set-up if you are making a presentation at the interview, especially if the presentation is electronic.	Dash in at the last minute and then spend the first ten minutes of your interview time fiddling with plugs and frantically typing commands.

Do	Don't
Take a paper copy of an electronic presentation … just in case.	Underestimate the power of showing you are prepared for the unexpected, e.g. technical breakdowns, interviewer being called away, a telephone ringing in the room when you are in full flow.
Turn off you mobile phone.	Forget!

▶ The Interviewer

Before the interview takes place, the interviewer needs to take some preparatory steps to ensure that the interview runs smoothly and that candidates are able to present themselves in the best light.

Before the Interview

As part of your preparation for the interview, you should give candidates clear directions to your company, parking details, if necessary, and an idea of how long the interview will take. If you expect the person to make a presentation, ensure that your expectations of length of presentation, type of presentation (PowerPoint, non-electronic, visual aids) and subject matter are well understood by the candidate before the day. Also ensure that if the presentation is to be electronic, you have a technical person standing by for set-up.

Be sure that you have booked a room for the correct amount of time. It is embarrassing for you and the person you are interviewing if a colleague knocks briskly on the door, enters and tells you, 'This room is booked for an important meeting, so I am afraid you'll have to move.' It doesn't create a good impression, wastes time and makes you and the interviewee feel uncomfortable.

You need to make time to read and review a CV, and have some questions planned that show you have looked at it. Also, be clear about the main points you need to address during the interview. If your company uses psychometric testing as part of the interview process, use it in conjunction with your face-to-face interview to assess the interviewee; neither disregard the information the test has given you nor rely on it totally. It will give you a good questioning base and enable you to make a considered judgement, particularly where interpersonal skills are concerned.

Interviews of any kind are two-way affairs. You should therefore expect the interviewee to ask questions about the company's vision for the future, company culture, training and development, and more in-depth questions about the role for which he or she is being interviewed. As the interviewer, you should be well versed in company knowledge, up to date on current growth patterns and products/services, and clear about the requirements for the job role and where the person will be working. If you are in doubt about any information you should know, take a colleague who has up-to-date facts into the interview with you.

Conducting the Interview

Don't be late for the interview. If you keep an interviewee waiting under the misapprehension that it makes you look important, it doesn't. It gives the impression that you are arrogant, unable to manage time and do not value the interviewee's time.

Always introduce yourself clearly when greeting the interviewee and ensure they are offered a drink. If it is lunchtime and you haven't had a chance to eat, wait until the interview is over before eating your sandwich. I have seen executives swing into an interview room complete with sandwich bag and coffee, give a hasty, 'Sorry I'm a bit late,' and then proceed to conduct the interview while consuming the contents of the sandwich bag, with no offer of refreshment to the interviewee and no real structure to the interview ... and no manners! It is important to explain to the interviewee at the start of the interview the format and structure that it will take, and also to reiterate how long you believe it will take.

If you haven't told the interviewee beforehand that a second (or even a third) person will be in the interview with you, then when you greet them you should, after pleasantries, tell them something along the lines of, 'I have asked John Johns, our Product Marketing Manager, to join us, as he has a detailed understanding of our new product range.' This will set the scene for the interviewee rather than just leaving them to wonder who the additional person is when you both enter the room.

During the interview be enthusiastic, listen closely to what is being said and maintain your level of interest, even if you have been interviewing all day and it is now 7.00 p.m. If you find four or more people in a day too tiring and your enthusiasm levels are on the downturn, ensure that you are more realistic in the future about how many people you can comfortably interview in a day. If you feel tired, you are not projecting yourself, and therefore your company, well. It is also unprofessional not to consider how your tired behaviour will affect the person you are interviewing: it will not give them the opportunity to present themselves in the best light if you aren't as attentive and enthusiastic as you should be.

While interviewing, you really don't want to make the inter- viewee feel any more nervous than they probably already are, so a relaxed style of questioning – a conversational style – will put people at ease. You do want to avoid questioning in a manner that could be interpreted as an interrogation; people tend to clam up if they feel inhibited, and an interrogation will make an interviewee feel very uncomfortable.

If you believe that the person you are interviewing seems right for the job, give encouraging signals, but if you know you never want to see them again, don't give them false hopes by saying that you will definitely be inviting them back for a second interview. It is perfectly acceptable to say that you have other candidates to see and that you will get back within a certain time frame.

Concluding the Interview

Bring the interview to an end within the timescale you set at the beginning. Thank the candidate for coming and walk with them to the lift or exit – saying you will be in touch or that you look forward to seeing them again, or even, 'See you on Monday.'

Whether the interviewee is successful or unsuccessful, always follow up with a letter. For the successful candidate a letter from you saying how much you are looking forward to working with them, or having them in the team – or both – will get your working relationship off to a positive start.

You should write this letter even if you have a human resources person to handle the package and details. For the unsuccessful person, a short note thanking the candidate for coming and saying briefly why they haven't been successful – such as lack of technical skills or unsuitable job expertise – is so much better than sending a letter that simply states, 'We regret to inform you that on this occasion you have been unsuccessful'.

Arranging a Second Interview

If you want to ask someone back for a second interview, explain why they are being asked back and who you would like them to see. Discuss with them when you plan to do second interviews and check their availability. If possible, decide on a date there and then. If that isn't practical, give the interviewee the date you will be back to them by and clarify how you will contact them to confirm arrangements.

When people come back for a second interview, you may be the second or even third person that the interviewee has seen, so make sure you know what questions have already been asked, what areas need qualification/testing further and what the interviewee has been told.

Do What You Say You Will

If you tell someone you will contact them to agree a date for the next interview, a follow-up discussion or a final decision, always make sure you do.

If you interview on a regular basis, you will have developed your own style and methods. For those of you who interview occasionally, the following checklist will jog your memory and act as a refresher.

CHECKLIST FOR INTERVIEWERS

Do	Don't
Give clear directions as to where the interview will be held and how to get to the building.	Assume the interviewee will know exactly where you are located.
Be clear about your expectations for the interview, particularly if a presentation is involved.	Spring surprises on the interviewee.
Book a room for the interview and tell colleagues you are interviewing.	Take calls or allow the interview to be interrupted.
Read the CV and any other relevant information, such as psychometric test results, beforehand and prepare questions accordingly.	Look at the CV for the first time during the interview.

Do	Don't
Listen and question in an empathetic manner.	Make the interviewee feel they are being interrogated.
Be well versed in your organisation's vision, achievements and products or services.	Try to bluff your way through. If you don't know something, ask someone to join the interview who does.
Be on time, well prepared and welcoming.	Rush in at the last minute with a pile of papers to shuffle through and just say, 'Oh, hello.'
Ask the interviewee if they would like a drink.	Take food into the interview room with you.
Be enthusiastic, listen carefully and maintain your interest levels.	Over-commit to too many interviews in one day. If you are tired, you will be perceived as being disinterested and unprofessional.
Give the right messages.	Give people false hopes or information.
Be informed for the second interview stage: check with colleagues for details and information.	Just do your own thing – you will waste time and make yourself and the company look foolish.
Contact the successful and unsuccessful interviewees by the time you have agreed.	Ignore the timescale you have agreed – it is rude and shows an arrogant and uncaring attitude.
Turn off your mobile phone during the interview.	Forget!

Once the job interview is over and decisions have been made, it is a sign of change and of new beginnings. Starting a job in a new company is one occasion when you need to consider what needs to be done to create the right impression. If you are beginning a new project or moving to a new role within a large organisation, you will be faced with similar challenges.

Initial Steps in Business

If you are beginning a new project, starting a new job or doing something different in your working life that you haven't attempted before, you may find yourself wondering how to cope or how to handle situations with style. The following general business etiquette (BE) tips and specific tips for managers will enable you to handle both the expected ... and the unexpected.

▶ Making Introductions

In business, introductions are quite straightforward, as men and women are treated as equals. There are three main categories:

You introduce: (a) A colleague to colleagues.
               (b) A junior position to a senior position.
               (c) A colleague to a customer.

If you are introducing colleagues at the same level within the company, you would probably say something along the lines of, 'Oh Carol, do you know Kevin Michaels? Kevin this is Carol Hoy, our new Marketing Manager.'

In every other situation, the correct order for introducing

people is to address the senior person first; for example, 'Mr Senior Position, may I introduce you to Mr Junior Position,' and 'Sam Junior this is Mrs Sue Senior, our managing director,' and 'Mr Customer, may I introduce a colleague of mine ...' The important thing to remember here is that even if the customer is 16 years of age and you are introducing them to your managing director, the customer is still more important than the managing director. The customer is seen to be in the senior position in this instance.

When introducing yourself, you simply say, 'How do you do' or, 'Good morning/good afternoon/good evening. My name is ...' Say who you are and, if appropriate, which company you are from. If you are at a large company meeting, it's worth giving your title and saying which department you are from.

Do not use courtesy titles when introducing yourself. Lady, Lord, Professor, Dr, Mr, Mrs, Miss and Ms are all courtesy titles.

Once introductions have been made, most people in business these days call one another by their first name, but if in doubt, do not immediately do so – use the appropriate courtesy title and surname; for example:

▶ 'Lynne, may I introduce you to Mrs Tina Breda.'

▶ 'How do you do Mrs Breda? How nice to see you here.'

▶ 'Please call me Tina, Lynne.'

▶ 'Thank you.'

A young man told me recently that it feels really strange for him to say, 'How do you do' and he would much prefer to say, 'Hi.' 'Hi' is fine if you are meeting in a very informal atmosphere. We are, however, talking business here, and if 'How do you do' is just too much for you, then 'Good morning/afternoon/evening' is as informal as you can be without appearing too casual.

To Rise or Not to Rise

In the workplace, whether you are male or female, you should always be on your feet when being introduced or if you are introducing someone. In social situations women, especially older women, would not be expected to stand to be introduced. In social situations men standing when women enter a room is still appreciated, particularly by older women. It very rarely happens in business now.

▶ Using Names Correctly

A point here about personal relationships in business: if you know the chief executive officer personally, don't flaunt it. If everyone else in the organisation calls her 'Mrs Adams' in public, so should you.

Many people dislike having their names abbreviated, so unless people introduce themselves as Dick rather than Richard, or Nic rather than Nicola, do use full names. If you hear a person called by a nickname or an obvious pet name, such as Kaz instead of Karen, or Jimbo instead of Jim, for example, don't automatically assume that you can address those people in the same manner.

Steer clear of using luv, pet, my dear, sweetheart and darlin' unless you have worked with people for ages and these idioms are used when greeting one another as part of the camaraderie. No matter how well you know one another and think you get on, always be wary of being overly familiar.

▶ Shaking Hands

There are many silent messages exchanged with a handshake. You should always offer a firm handshake that is not crushing or limp.

▶ A direct palm-on-palm handshake is open and welcoming and is the one to use.

▶ A palm offered in a downwards position shows a dominant aggressive nature.

▶ A palm offered in an upwards position signifies a submissive nature.

There are psychological advantages to be gained by moving forward and offering your hand to initiate a handshake: you are perceived as being keen to put others at ease, friendly and welcoming. Pumping a hand can become an embarrassment – an absolute maximum of three times is quite enough. If you are on the receiving end of a pumper, simply grasp their wrist gently with your left hand; it looks friendly and immediately stops the pumping action.

▶ Kissing and Hugging

Greeting people you know in business can be difficult. If you've known someone for a long time, then a hug or a peck on the cheek between men and women is quite normal. It is important to be discrete, however, and if others are around who aren't in the hugging circle, then I would definitely say shake a person's hand and show your pleasure in seeing them in the warmth of your greeting and facial expression.

Men should certainly not assume that they can automatically kiss a woman. And if women greet other women with loud screeches and hugs this knocks their credibility sideways. If in any doubt, shake hands and smile warmly.

▸Remembering Names

How many of us are really good at remembering names when we are introduced to people? It does make a person feel good if you remember their name. A technique I use is to repeat the name when a person is introduced to me. For example, 'How do you do – my name is Diana Bradley.' 'How do you do, Diana Bradley? It's good to meet you.' Always try to say both the first name and surname; that way you stand a much better chance of remembering at least one name. If you are at a meeting in which unfamiliar people are sitting around a table, a useful technique is to draw the shape of the table on your notepad and, as people introduce themselves, jot down their names in the spot where they are sitting, as shown in the example below:

Meeting with John O'Connell's team, 4 July 2002

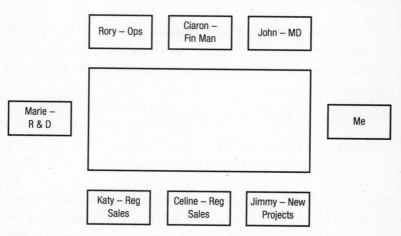

This acts as a good *aide-mémoire* while in the meeting. If you have to write a report or need to contact people afterwards, you can refer to your table plan and visualise people; this makes recalling what they said easier.

If you do forget a name, apologise and ask for it again. You do need to listen carefully. The problem with most of us is that we are too busy making our 30-second judgement of a person and not listening properly to names as we are being introduced. If you listen, you will remember names and details.

▶ Sending Greetings by E-mail and Memo

If you have moved departments, or started a new job or project, it is unrealistic to expect everyone to know who you are and where you are in your new role. Make sure your e-mails and memos include your full name, title and contact numbers.

▶ Need to Knows

When you are new to a company and it doesn't have an induction programme or a human-resource person to guide you through the 'need to knows', make sure you speak to a person in authority and define from the start what the policies are on the following:

▶ Personal telephone and e-mail restrictions.

▶ Arrival and departure times.

▶ Security.

▶ Dress conventions (does the company have dress-down days; do men have to wear suit jackets all the time; are trousers on women frowned upon?).

▶ Home usage of equipment and stationery.

▶ Other 'need to knows' specific to your job role.

Here is a quick checklist to ensure your working relationships get off to a good start.

CHECKLIST FOR THE NEWCOMER

Do	Don't
Introduce yourself to others.	Expect others always to remember to introduce you.
Introduce a junior person/position to a senior person/position.	Forget that customers and suppliers are treated as senior.
Say, 'How do you do,' 'Good morning/afternoon/evening' when being introduced or introducing yourself.	Just say, 'Allo.'
Say who you are and what you do or which company you are from when introducing yourself.	Use courtesy titles when introducing yourself.
Stand to greet and introduce yourself and others in business, whether you are male or female.	Expect older women to stand to be introduced in social situations.
Offer a direct palm-to-palm, firm handshake.	Offer a hand with a palm in a downwards or upwards position.
Move forward and offer your hand to initiate a handshake.	Be a pumper – a maximum of three pumps is enough!
Repeat a name when introduced so that you remember it; repeat it once or twice again in the conversation that follows.	Use the person's name continuously – at the end of every sentence.
Make sure your e-mails and memos have your full name, title and contact numbers on them when you are new to a job, department or project.	Assume everyone will know who you are and what you do if you don't tell them.

Do	Don't
Check out the human-resources policies when you are new to an organisation.	Wait to be told about 'need to knows' – it is your responsibility to find out.

▶ Becoming a Successful Manager

If you are in a management role or aspiring to management, to gain credibility from the beginning – in a new role, company, project or situation – you need to consider more than just doing your job. The higher up the career ladder you go, the more open to criticism you become. It is therefore essential to develop your interpersonal skills continuously.

When you are managing new situations, you need to behave in a confident manner in order to make people feel inspired and motivated.

Managing New Situations

The impact you have on the people working for you takes place very quickly. Within the first week, people will be reacting to what you say and how you say it in either a negative or a positive manner. The aim here is to make sure you always get a positive reception.

Many managers starting a new role completely forget the people they have working for them because they are so keen to impress with how they can deliver figures and show their expertise. Yes, performance is important, but it will be the best it can be if the people working for you are given clear objectives and know what you expect of them. They also need to know that they can rely on your support while achieving those expect-ations.

Introducing Yourself

As soon as you know you are on the move, get a list of the names, functions and extensions of the people who will be working for you. Take time to see each person – if it is feasible – or department. People need to feel that their boss wants to know them and what they are doing. By introducing yourself and listening to them, you begin to indicate that they are important to you and the success of the department; it makes people feel valued and that's a good feeling. When people feel good, they are better motivated to achieve success.

Initiating Changes

Your way of doing things will be different from your predecessor's because you have a different personality. If you have to make changes to processes and procedures straight away, involve as many relevant people as possible to work with you. Brainstorming sessions that result in actions scheduled to be achieved by certain dates, with responsibilities given to individuals, will ensure that you build a team approach for dealing with any change or new project. Failing to take people into your confidence and giving the impression that you have all the answers and can achieve objectives without working with others will cause resentment and resistance.

Managing ... Everything

There may well be occasions, particularly when you are the new man or woman, when all sorts of problems will find their way to your desk – anything from heating levels to office tidiness. Encourage people to say what they believe needs to be done to put the problem right: what actions would they take to see that the problem is overcome? By encouraging people to come to you with a solution, you will be developing their skills. It's also a good way of ensuring that you aren't expected to have an answer for everything, and that you are delegating too.

Delivering a Difficult Message

Management is challenging and some of the tasks you are expected to do aren't pleasant. So often an unpleasant task has to be carried out within the first few months of starting in a new role. If you do have a difficult message to deliver to your workforce, then for goodness sake say so. That way your body language will be in sync with the spoken word. Beginning a sentence with, 'This is a difficult message for me to deliver' isn't weak; it's powerful because you are telling the truth. Your audience, be it one person or hundreds, will find you credible and sincere.

Dealing with Animosity

If you sense the presence of animosity or restrictive attitudes, they need to be dealt with as soon as possible. The longer tensions are left to fester, the more difficult they are to handle. Get the people with the difficult attitudes together and ask them what their issues and concerns are. Also ask them what they believe needs to be done to improve the atmosphere and situation. Then agree with them who will do what and by when, and arrange a follow-up meeting to monitor progress.

Keeping Notes

As a manager, networking is a skill that has to be high up on your agenda. If you work in a large organisation, you will need to begin networking immediately you are on board. Working with a large number of people makes it difficult to remember individual circumstances. Make notes in your diary reminding you to ask about personal situations, important events, new projects or issues people may have mentioned to you. It's a simple method of remembering – and it works.

The best managers start the way they mean to go on. This checklist for managers will ensure your beginnings will be positive.

CHECKLIST FOR NEW MANAGERS

Do	Don't
Make time to get to know each department and, where feasible, each person.	Believe that impressing people with technical expertise is more important than listening and working with them.
Organise brainstorming sessions to gain information and commitment.	Ignore people's opinions – it will build resentment and resistance.
Encourage people to think for themselves.	Expect to have the answers to all of the problems all of the time.
Deliver a difficult message in an honest manner: you build credibility.	Say one thing when your body language is saying something else: you confuse your audience and don't build trust.
Deal with animosity and undercurrents as soon as possible. Deal with and monitor the situation through to a healthy conclusion.	Let atmospheres fester.
Network and develop strong business relationships with people at all levels and across all disciplines.	Ignore the development of your interpersonal skills.

Regardless of your position in an organisation, your greatest challenge will be how to communicate well in any given situation. You may find communicating from a distance a particular challenge. Technology is developing at a rapid pace, and it has to impact on the speed at which we send and receive information over distance. You therefore need to be aware of the appropriate means of communication to use if you are to deliver quality customer service.

CHAPTER 7

Communicating from a Distance

Your ability to communicate effectively by telephone and via the written word is an essential skill for today's workplace. Most of us would be lost without our telephone, mobile phone, e-mail and fax facilities. Today, the ability to write a good business letter is often overlooked. E-mails are so informal and fast that most of us will automatically use them as our number-one choice, unless we need to respond to a customer's request, attach a covering letter to a proposal or respond officially to a complaint. I have no intention of taking you through a written communication or telephone skills course here. I will, however, give you some tips on how to project yourself well on the telephone, and cover some of the pitfalls to avoid when writing.

▶ Using the Telephone

As is the case with any form of people interaction, the first impression you give is all-important when you answer the telephone. Why? Because the ability to answer a telephone well initiates a positive reaction from the caller, which gives both you and your company immediate credibility.

Taking Calls for a Company

If you are a receptionist taking calls and transferring them to others throughout an organisation, you are your company's first impression. The challenge for any receptionist is to transfer people quickly and cheerfully. That includes keeping waiting callers happy during those times when a telephone extension just keeps ringing because the person who owns it has disappeared without activating their voicemail or answerphone, or hasn't asked some-one else to take their calls while they are away from their desk.

Keeping your tone of voice bright and cheerful under these circumstances can be difficult, but it is essential to do so, as the caller can be easily put off or become disgruntled if a heavy sigh is transmitted down the line and an agitated voice states in an off-hand manner, 'There's nobody there at the moment.' A receptionist should always try to remain calm and positive, however pressurised the job. Any hint of irritation or stress is immediately sensed by callers, with potentially very negative consequences for the company.

Taking Your Own Calls

Many of you don't have the luxury of having someone else filter or manage telephone calls for you. If you have a direct-line system, then each time you answer your phone you are making a first impression. Some companies insist on:

A greeting: 'Good morning'/'Good afternoon.'

The name of the company: 'Business Etiquette International.'

The name of the person: 'Lynne Brennan speaking.'

A further greeting: 'How may/can I help you?'

If people feel comfortable with saying all of that, it sounds professional and welcoming. I think most of us have a problem with too long a greeting and it can sound contrived. The important point here is to be clear and to let the caller know who is answering the telephone. Use two names. A bright, 'Good morning, Lynne Brennan speaking,' sounds far more welcoming and professional than, 'Good morning, Lynne here.'

Be aware of how you come across to others in a situation such as this: you are right in the middle of a task; the telephone rings; you snatch at it and answer in automatic-pilot mode, probably breathing out as you do so. Not impressive, is it? In fact, it makes the caller feel unwanted. OK they aren't, but if you are in the middle of working and you don't want to be interrupted, put your telephone on to answerphone or voicemail, or divert it to a colleague, until you are at a point where you can take calls without feeling irritated.

Body language on the phone? Yes, the way you sit or stand will affect your tone of voice. If you are slumped over a desk, you are inhibiting your ability to breathe properly and your voice will lack enthusiasm. If you sit up, your voice tone will sound far more positive and energised.

If you do have a difficult situation to deal with or you are feeling uncomfortable – nervous, angry or frustrated – in any way about delivering a message, your voice tone will sound agitated if you sit down and fidget with discomfort. Stand up. You'll be surprised at how much better you feel. You can breathe deeply and pace around the room if need be – you'll feel more in control and your delivery will be far more effective.

Using Answerphones

The use of an answerphone or voicemail, or both, is now accepted and almost expected in the workplace. If you use an answerphone to cover for you when you are away from your desk, make sure your recording is simple and to the point, and that it encourages people to leave you a message. If people do leave messages, return their calls!

Using Voicemail

A voicemail capability on a telephone system is a versatile and efficient means of ensuring that people know where you are and how long it will be before they can expect a reply from you or be able to speak to you – if used properly! Many people record a message on the day the system is set up, and that's it. This is not very efficient, nor is it the way voicemail is meant to be used.

Take the example of a favourite bank manager I know. His voicemail is updated daily and says exactly where he'll be and until when and who can help in his absence. When a message is left, he deals with it upon his return. His voice is normal – you actually feel as if he is speaking to you because it isn't stilted, but neither does it sound robotic. Using a voicemail facility correctly enables you to make better use of your time and to stay in touch, even when you have a hectic schedule.

Telephone Conferencing

For those of you who are members of remote teams (sales people and those who work from home), and for those working in the international workplace, telephone conferences can be an everyday occurrence. They enable you to keep in touch with clients and colleagues and cut down on time delays when urgent decisions have to be made. Their one big disadvantage is that people listening to you speaking cannot see your face.

It is therefore essential not to make tongue-in-cheek or demeaning remarks while telephone conferencing. What you say to colleagues face to face can be taken out of context when they cannot see the wry smile on your face or the raised eyebrow and grin.

Your tone of voice needs to be enthusiastic and lively and your message clear. Pronouncing the ends of words makes it easier for people to listen and understand you.

Your ability to listen to others is certainly put to the test when a conference call isn't chaired properly. There is nothing worse than attending a conference call where people overtalk one another; it means that they are not listening to each other.

If you are asked to be part of a conference call, make sure you 'sign in' on time; it's irritating for others to have to wait for one person before the purpose of the conference call can be discussed. Your reputation will suffer if you are always the person who is late joining the call.

Using Mobile Phones

These miracles of technology are such a necessary part of our working and social lives (for some people they appear as attachments to their hands and ears) that most of us find it difficult to imagine how we managed without them. The miniature mobile phone's microphones enable the transmission of soft voices over thousands of miles, so why do people insist on shouting into them? If you shout, nearly everyone within earshot will become very agitated and view you and the mobile phone as a pervasive nuisance.

A mobile phone has an 'on' and 'off' button for a purpose, and some people don't use the 'off' button often enough! It is essential to disable the ringer of a mobile phone and switch on the call diversion or message facility before going into a meeting of any kind. The only exception to this rule is if people within the meeting are *all* expecting a call to be made and have agreed the call should be taken. Some people switch their mobile phone to vibrate believing that this is less disruptive; any of you who have witnessed a vibrating mobile phone whiz across a meeting-room table know that isn't true.

If you do forget to turn off your mobile and it rings at an inopportune moment, at least make sure you know where it is so that you don't have to spend embarrassing seconds, which seem like hours, searching for it. Apologise. Don't try to see who is contacting you before turning it off. Just switch it off.

Using Text Messaging

This has to be the briefest type of communication that you will come across. Used mainly from colleague to colleague at the moment, it is a fun way to send messages. It has a language of its own and unless you know a customer understands the lingo, don't think of sending them a text message. If you do text message colleagues (and customers), be wary of sending a message late at night. You may think the message will be read in the morning, but as many mobile phones are permanently switched on you could receive a very rude reply.

Here are a few text-language phrases that you can use to shorten messages:

FWIT	for what it's worth
IIRC	if I recall correctly
HTH	happy to help/hope that helps
TIA	thanks in advance
FYI	for your information
BTW	by the way
OBO	our best offer
TTYL	talk to you later
BCNU	be seeing you
CU2MO	see you tomorrow
IMHO	in my humble opinion

And there's more. The following visual clues are known as smilies – you enter the symbols and faces appear on the screen:

:-)	=	smiling
:-(	=	frowning
:-D	=	surprised
:-/	=	perplexed

Smilies enable you to communicate how you feel about a subject. They can appear to be flippant, so be really sure that you are sending them in the right context and to a person who is sure to understand and appreciate them.

▶ Using Videoconferencing

This is slightly different from your normal expectation of a telephone, I'll grant you. Speaking to people via a video-conference needs good interpersonal skills. People see as well as hear your frustration or approval when you make a point. Make sure your silent and spoken communication skills are 'speaking' the same message.

Talking of messages, don't start a conversation on the side while another person is speaking – it is rude and ignorant. Try to avoid moving around too much when sitting at a video-conference meeting; the technology will make you look robotic. If you continuously fidget and draw attention to yourself, you will make an impression – of the wrong kind.

▶ Using E-mails

As is the case with mobile phones, most of us wonder how we communicated effectively – especially across time zones – before e-mailing became commonplace in the workplace. However, there are times when I wonder whether people ever stop to think before sending an e-mail.

E-mailing Groups of People

Think before you send. Messages such as, 'The sandwich lady is here,' are e-mailed to all and sundry in large organisations with no consideration given to who actually works in the office and who works from home. I can appreciate that typing five words, pressing send and distributing to an organisation's address book may appear to be a quick way of passing information to as many people as possible, but in my view the most sensible thing to do would be to arrange for the sandwich lady to be at the premises daily at a certain time. Put notices up on noticeboards to that effect, and if an e-mail is necessary, then distribute one – once. This saves time and is more efficient.

I have actually seen an e-mail arrive in America telling a whole office there that the sandwich lady has arrived in a London office. It does make the person who sent it appear inefficient – they can become the butt of jokes and will be known internationally for all the wrong reasons!

Adding Subject Lines

Become an expert at summarising the content of your e-mail in a few words on the subject line. It helps people prioritise their response and find the message afterwards. Here are a few tips:

▶ Be specific. Rather than 'Your advice needed,' make it 'Advice on transport needed.'

▶ Change the subject. When you reply to a message but want to introduce a new subject, don't forget to change the subject line. Otherwise it can be confusing and makes filing difficult.

▶ Use a new message for a new thread. If you need to change the topic entirely, it's usually best to send a new message, allowing the receiver to file it separately.

Copying People

Another point to consider before your message wings its way across cyberspace is who to copy a message to. More often than not people tend to copy far too many people. Unless you happen to be working on an extremely large project or are responsible for relaying a message that *everyone* in the company needs to see, keep the cc-ing down to a minimum. Those who try to impress by copying people up, sideways, down and internationally, rarely do.

E-mail Style

When writing an e-mail, unless you have to get a formal response to someone quickly and it is virtually a copy of a letter you will post later in the day, you should use a written-conversation style. So your greeting can be anything (polite, that is) from: 'Hi', 'Hello', 'Good morning Peter', or 'Suzy', through to the more formal: 'Dear Claire Zoller', 'Dear Mr O'Sullivan' or 'Sir/Madam' to name but a few.

To sign off, people tend to say, 'Speak to you later', 'Look forward to seeing you', 'Thanks', 'Bye for now', 'Cheers' or simply finish the message and write their name. If you do write a more formal message, then match the sign-off to the salutation: the sign-offs for 'Dear Claire Zoller' and 'Dear Mr O'Sullivan' would be 'Yours sincerely', and for 'Dear Sir/Madam' 'Yours faithfully' is appropriate.

Particularly in large organisations, it's helpful to include your name with your return e-mail address, as in: marketing@foto-suppliers.etc.co (Len Scap). It's also useful to add a signature block: six lines at the end of your e-mail that contain your department or function, your telephone and fax numbers and, if necessary, your full address.

Bear in mind that using all upper case type can make an e-mail awkward to read, and purists relate it to shouting.

Interpreting the Message

If you are e-mailing between different cultures, think about what you say and how you say it. Dry humour, sarcasm and cynical remarks do not translate well to a person whose first language isn't English.

I worked with a multinational company a few years ago that employed teams of engineers in Scandinavia and the UK. There was a breakdown in communication and team spirit because the UK engineers were e-mailing the Scandinavians in exactly the same way as they e-mailed one another. The Scandinavians didn't appreciate 'the aside comments' being made, because their humour was different. By the same token, the Scandinavians requested details and plans in what the Brits interpreted as a command; for example, 'Send us the latest changes on Project C'.

By simply leaving the humour out of the Brits' e-mails and asking the Scandinavians to request and add 'please' rather than issuing commands, the communication and team spirit improved dramatically within a very short space of time.

With so much interaction in business between Britain and the United States, many of you will have experienced the differences in spelling and interpretations of certain words. George Bernard Shaw wasn't wrong when he made his famous remark, 'England and America are two countries divided by a common language.'

As e-mail is the main method of communication with the United States nowadays, particularly in large organisations, be aware of the fact that when setting dates or dating documentation, the month always comes before the date; for example, when writing 3 January 2003 in numerals, 3.1.2003 is used in Britain, whereas 1.3.2003 is used in America. You may hear people say, 'But that's the way we do it here in Britain.' Yes, that is correct, but you can see how confusion could arise if we stuck to 'our way of doing things'. What we interpret as 3 January would mean 1 March in America.

One of the many times I have used a word with a different meaning in the United States was when I was working with a human-resources department at a Seattle-based company. We were eating lunch together. As it was near Christmas, we began discussing gifts we were buying for family and friends. I said I was particularly pleased to have found a casket of chocolates to give to an elderly aunt. The looks on my fellow diners' faces were quite incredulous. One asked, 'A casket?'

'Yes,' I replied, 'it's really pretty; it's decorated with gold handles.' Yet more looks of consternation.

'How big is it?' another person asked.

'Oh, about 12 inches long by 6 inches wide,' I replied, 'It's really just a pretty box holding about one pound of really yummy chocolates.' Much shrieking and laughter. A casket in America is a coffin! That goof didn't impact on my business in a negative way because I was there and able to explain what I meant. Imagine the chaos it could have caused if I had e-mailed an American client telling them a casket of chocolates was on its way!

Before You Hit 'Send'

If you are angry or upset with a person, you may well spend ten minutes writing an e-mail venting your feelings. It will probably make you feel better, but you will regret sending such a message and others will see you as overreacting and out of control. Do not hit 'send' in anger.

▶ When you are e-mailing, always ensure you are polite, that you check spelling and that the information you are about to send makes sense. It's so easy to miss out words or type complete gobbledygook when you are rushing to finish something.

▶ Be discreet: never e-mail sensitive or really confidential infor- mation. A recipient, as well as you, could be embarrassed if a confidential message got misrouted.

▸ Be concise – numbered bullet points enable people to read an e-mail quickly, and that is really appreciated when your incoming e-mails number 50-plus a day.

OK, you can hit 'send' now.

And when You are on the Receiving End ...

Are you one of those people who find it impossible to clear their e-mails on a daily basis? I'm not surprised if you are. If you work for a large organisation, it must be a nightmare some days. I was talking to a client only last week who'd been out of the office for three days and logged on to find 160 e-mails waiting for him to read and answer. Many of you will identify with that situation. It's frustrating when you know that over half of such a large number of e-mails are out of date or irrelevant. Even deleting so many takes time. If you have the opportunity to suggest that people *think* before they send an e-mail, it will save you and your organisation time and money.

▸ Sending Faxes

Faxing is not as popular now that e-mail has invaded our lives, but faxes are still important pieces of equipment, and organisations rely on them a great deal. When writing a fax message there is no need to write, 'Dear John' and sign off, 'Yours sincerely' – it is not a letter. You simply write your message and sign it personally if possible.

Fax machines are really useful. However, if you have an office at home and a marketing company decides to do a fax mailing at two o'clock in the morning, the whirring and bleeping isn't my idea of good marketing or business etiquette (BE). So if you are a marketing company who believe a middle-of-the-night fax mailing is a good way of promoting your organisation, you are selfish and wrong.

For those of you who suffer from fax-marketing overload, you can subscribe to a fax-banning service – that way you'll sleep better and save a few trees!

▶ Writing Business Letters

A well-written letter projects personal and business credibility. Receiving such a letter shows that care and consideration have been taken by the writer. If a letter is laid out well and the content follows a logical sequence, it makes it easier to read and remember.

Dear ... Yours ...

When writing to a person in an official capacity with whom you have no personal relationship, start the letter with 'Dear Sir' or 'Dear Madam' and end it with 'Yours faithfully'.

▶ For a new acquaintance – contacted by letter only, start the letter with either 'Dear Paul Rose' or 'Dear Mr Rose'.

▶ For everyone else who you have established a rapport with, unless you know a person would be offended, start the letter with 'Dear Will'; for someone who might be offended by this, start with 'Dear Mr Duncan'.

▶ In both cases you can end with 'Yours sincerely', or 'With kindest regards', or 'With best wishes'. You can also end with 'With best wishes, Yours sincerely', but it isn't necessary to use the two – it's your choice.

Making Yourself Clear

Try to project your personality when writing a letter. Use words that are clear and avoid verbose statements – why use two words when one will do? Let me give you an example: instead of writing, 'Subsequent to our meeting of 4 July …', which sounds pompous and dated, write, 'After our meeting on 4 July …'. It sounds crisper and more natural.

Before You Post It

The last sentence of any business letter should indicate what will happen next. Once you have reached this stage, read through the letter to check that the tone of it will bring the required response. Check for spelling and grammatical errors. We take software checkers so much for granted these days, but a last read through and check before you sign a letter is a must. And remember to sign it! Make sure your name is typed under your signature. If your signature is anything like my husband's, you really wouldn't be able to guess what his name is from the signature, so a typed version of the name is a must. For women, if you want to give people a clue to your status, add in brackets, Mrs, Miss or Ms.

If you ensure that every letter you write has the human touch, and is clear, to the point and courteous, you show a commitment to producing quality documents – you'll be surprised at how many people will follow your lead.

Replying Promptly

When you are the receiver of a letter, do reply as promptly as possible – to ignore any correspondence is discourteous. When you ignore a letter, you ignore a person. The perception could be that you are too busy to be bothered and that's arrogant. Even if you have a hectic schedule, make time to reply to all your letters. If a person writes *to you*, they expect a reply *from you*.

▶ Sending Personal Notes

It is always essential to say thank you in writing when you have enjoyed another company's hospitality. Do so quickly on company paper. Other circumstances are:

▶ If you have been taken to lunch or wined and dined by an individual and it was a business meeting, then thanking the person on company paper is acceptable. More courteous and personal is a handwritten note or a 'blank', appropriate greetings card.

▶ When you hear that a colleague has been promoted, a handwritten message or greetings card is more personal and meaningful than an e-mail, but make sure the picture is appropriate or the gesture could backfire on you.

▶ When you hear of a business acquaintance's success, a handwritten note – not on company paper – will always be remembered.

▶ Using Compliments Slips

Items sent between business colleagues where little or no comment is needed should be accompanied by a compliments slip. If more than two sentences are needed, a letter should be written. Although most compliments slips have 'With Compliments' printed on them, a short message and signature, or a full signature, should be added.

If you handwrite business information in haste on a compliments slip, make sure you photocopy it before sending it.

Whatever method of communication you use, make sure that *you* are recognised by the listener or reader. The message from BE is simple – be clear, concise and human.

Here are some quick memory joggers to ensure distance will not hamper the way you communicate.

Communication Checklist

Do	Don't
Answer the telephone in a clear and bright manner and be aware of your body language.	Sigh into a telephone or slump over a desk while answering – your voice will lack energy.
Ask if it is convenient to speak when you make a telephone call.	Make lengthy personal calls on a regular basis.
Make sure your answerphone message encourages others to leave a message.	Record a message on the day the facility is set up and leave it.
Get back to people when they leave you a message.	Ignore messages.
Make the most of a voicemail facility and update your message on a regular basis.	Overtalk people – you won't be listening if you do.
Arrive on time for a conference call.	Get a bad reputation for always keeping people waiting.
Take advantage of technology by speaking at a normal level.	Talk loudly or shout into a mobile phone.
Switch off your mobile phone when attending any meeting unless others attending have agreed that you may take an expected call.	Bury your mobile phone in your briefcase during a meeting, just in case you have forgotten to turn it off. Rummaging around for your phone looks really unprofessional.

Do	Don't
Use texting between colleagues.	Assume everyone will understand the lingo.
Think before sending an e-mail.	Copy e-mails to all and sundry.
Write an e-mail in a conversational manner.	Shout, by using upper case throughout your message.
Be aware of how words and humour are interpreted.	Believe that everyone will understand you if you ignore cultural differences.
Be discrete.	E-mail sensitive or confidential information – it could be misrouted.
Try to influence the e-mail culture in your company to eliminate unnecessary e-mailing.	E-mail the person sitting next to you with a 'Are you coming to lunch' message!
Make sure your business letters are well laid out and follow a logical sequence.	Use verbose and pompous statements.
Reply promptly to any correspondence.	Ignore letters.
Send handwritten notes to congratulate colleagues and business acquaintances on successes.	Use company headed paper for personal letters.
Check any form of written communication before sending it.	Ever write a message or letter when you feel frustrated or angry.

The one sure thing about BE is that it will prepare you for almost any situation you have to deal with in your working life and, as you will notice, the skills will transfer easily into everyday-life situations in or out of work. As you read this, some of you may be on your way to meet a person or a group of people to discuss business for your company, a charity you work with or a community project. On the other hand, many of you may be 'meetinged out'!

CHAPTER 8

Productive Meetings

Have you ever suffered from meeting fatigue? You may have experienced days full of one meeting after another, most of them not starting on time because you have to wait for a single person, even more of them not particularly well run, with no actions resulting from them and no follow-up to previous actions. Let me guess how many heads will be bobbing in agreement. Too many, I suspect.

So why is it that people attend meetings to report and review, to share information and listen to briefings, to be part of a decision-making process, yet *still* there are communication problems within organisations?

▶ Avoiding Common Pitfalls

I believe companies (including each person who ever attends a meeting within a company) fall into traps. Let me try to release those traps and hopefully prevent many of you from falling into them.

I'll use a checklist approach as you may wish to adapt this to ensure your meetings are always effective, beginning *before the meeting takes place.*

Before the Meeting – when You are the Arranger

▸ Firstly, before you do anything, check the objectives. If there are no clear objectives, there is no clear purpose in holding a meeting – so don't.

▸ When the objectives are clear, there is a purpose. Knowing what you need to achieve is great, but how long you need to achieve it is the big question. So many meetings begin well but lose focus on the way. This mainly happens because a time limit hasn't been considered, or a totally unrealistic time limit is incurred because the policy is, 'Meetings should take an hour, maximum!' Consider what type of meeting yours needs to be and how long you will need to achieve the objectives.

▸ Ask *only* the people who will progress the objectives of the meeting to attend.

▸ Prepare an agenda or an outline of what will be covered in the meeting, with a timescale, and send it to attendees beforehand wherever possible. Be sure to put the start and finish time on the agenda and stress that the meeting will begin promptly.

Before the Meeting – when You are the Invited

▸ If there is no obvious purpose or agenda, ask what the purpose is.

▸ If you have any doubts about the relevance of your attendance, you need to discuss it with the invitee and decide together whether or not you really need to attend.

▸ If you believe a colleague would be able to contribute more effectively, recommend they go in your place.

▸ Let the person arranging the meeting know whether you will be there or not, as soon as you can.

During the Meeting

▸ Arrive prepared and ready to begin the meeting at the stated time.

▸ Be clear and concise when putting forward your ideas and contributions – don't ramble on. You may like to consider using the 'past, present and future technique' here (*see page 48*). It's useful when you have to up-date the meeting's participants on a project or put forward new ideas.

▸ Respect other people's viewpoints – don't demean people if they have different views from yours.

▸ Be open to incorporating other people's ideas. When suggestions are made, don't overreact if you have put forward an idea and someone adds to it. Relax – don't see it as somebody muscling in. Accept and work with the suggestion and person.

▸ Do not go off at tangents: reminiscing about how things *used* to be isn't productive, and if there are only two of you at the meeting who remember the 'good old days', you run the risk of being put into the 'boring' category.

▸ Explain jargon and abbreviations. Don't assume everyone will know what you are talking about. If you are technical, don't go into a detailed explanation unless you know everyone in the meeting will understand you. Always qualify abbreviations, such as 'and the QC is fine', meaning 'quality control' in this instance, but it could mean something very different.

▸ Do not waste time with irrelevant interruptions or overtalking.

▶ Listen and observe how people react to what is being said. Knowing looks and sly grins show arrogance and bully tactics. If you listen well and disagree with something that has been said, say so; there's no point in having a second meeting outside the planned one, just to slate a colleague when an issue could have been overcome had it been faced up to at the appropriate time. Many people also pretend to be listening and then get caught out when asked a question, so pay attention to what is being said.

▶ When questioning or criticising other people's ideas or proposals, be courteous. So often people question or criticise in a manner that is aggressive and unnecessary. I was working with a group of very bright people recently who appeared incredibly arrogant simply because of their questioning technique. They had a real jugular-attacking approach. If you are faced with this, keep calm, answer any questions in an authoritative manner and don't let others make you feel uneasy – they are the ones who are insecure and out of control.

▶ Do not leave a meeting without being sure that you know what is expected of you and when you are expected to produce any actioned material.

▶ Behaving Appropriately at Meetings

Regardless of whether you chair, manage, facilitate or attend meetings of any kind, be aware of how your behaviour impacts on others. In the same way that a positive person encourages others, a negative person can have an alarmingly gloomy effect on those around them. Sometimes we are totally unaware of how negative body language impacts on others at a meeting. Here are just a few behaviours I've observed over the years and, believe me, they irritate, frustrate and ... just don't be the person who engages in any of them:

▶ Pen clicking.

▶ Shaking a leg in a nervous-twitch fashion.

▶ Looking at the ceiling while someone is talking.

▶ Pointing a pen when you speak to someone.

▶ Sighing loudly.

▶ Keeping your head down and picking your nails or concentrating intently on something you are fiddling with, such as a rubber, pencil or Blu-Tak.

▶ Raising your eyebrows when a suggestion is made but not following it up with a comment.

... and there are many more, but I'm sure you've got the gist.

▶ Chairing or Managing a Meeting

Chairing or managing a meeting is an art and a skill that needs to be developed if meetings are always to be productive. It is a skill that any manager needs in order to be recognised as a person who can control, encourage and deal with challenging situations, because that is what chairing a meeting is all about.

For those of you who have chaired meetings for years, forgive me if I state the obvious on occasions, but it is an understatement to say that I have witnessed some very poorly run meetings by very experienced managers.

The following tips should guide you and enhance your meetings:

▶ Always start a meeting on time.

▶ Tell people at the beginning of the meeting what the purpose is and what the agenda will cover, how much discussion time you estimate for each agenda item and when the meeting will finish.

▶ Ensure everyone knows one another. If new people are attending, ensure they are properly introduced.

▶ Review any previous meeting's action points and, where necessary, agree further dated actions – this is a stage that is very often overlooked. (What is the point of producing action lists if they are not followed through?)

▶ Keep to the agenda, or the purpose of the meeting becomes null and void.

▶ Ensure that everyone attending the meeting becomes involved.

▶ Be firm but friendly in controlling discussion, and make sure that no one person is allowed to dominate.

▶ If you sense dissention or animosity, address it in a purposeful manner.

▶ Be aware of secondary conversations and stop them.

▶ Keep the meeting on track and on time.

▶ If there is an item that obviously needs longer discussion time, either agree a time and place for a meeting to discuss it yourself, or give the responsibility to another person to arrange a separate meeting.

▶ Go through the action points and responsibilities and ensure that people know what is expected of them.

▶ Decide who needs to know and the best method of communicating the results of the meeting.

▸ If there is sensitive information under discussion, which cannot be spoken about until a decision has been made, agree how the 'no comment' message can be communicated.

▸ Agree the date and place of any follow-up meeting.

▸ Agree who will type up and circulate the action points, and by when.

▸ Thank people for attending and for their contribution.

▸ Finish on time.

▸ The Briefing Approach

For managers handling major changes in their business or changes in procedures, or those who need to give an overview and update of current projects to a team or group of people, you might consider the briefing approach. Here is a quick guide to introducing briefings to your workplace.

Preparing for the Meeting

▸ Plan well ahead, giving people good notification of when the briefing is to be held.

▸ Choose people to work with you who would deliver the best message about a particular topic – they needn't be a manager to do that.

▸ Set out clear time constraints.

▸ Tell people what you hope to achieve and your expectations from these briefing sessions.

▸ Consider how you or others will deal with negative issues.

▸ Be prepared with diagrams and back-up material.

At the Meeting

▸ Determine at the first meeting how frequently people feel future meetings need to be held.

▸ Have a combined agenda and action list for each meeting – it could look something like this:

AGENDA AND ACTION LIST

Agenda item	Action items	Responsibility
Business up-date		
Customer service problems		
Internal communication		
Training programmes		
Company news		

▸ Ensure that someone other than management is responsible for recording action points and responsibilities. A good rule is to have no more than one action item per topic per meeting.

▸ Loads of actions look great, but when you do the reality check, how many actions can you handle? It is important not to raise expectations to a level that is unrealistic – people will be disappointed and you don't often get a second chance, so always do what you say you will.

▶ Whoever is presenting needs to be clear and concise with their message without being abrupt and officious. Just standing up and telling a group of people what is going on will not achieve good communication, so there does need to be a 'checking for understanding'. The benefit of briefings is that you get feedback from your audience, whereas if you communicate only via the written word, there is less likelihood of really knowing how people feel.

▶ Timing needs to be controlled. If your briefing session is taking place during a lunch hour, allow time for people to eat, listen and question. You don't want a group of people to just listen – you *do* want to hear their opinions and encourage them to ask questions. One of the values of this type of meeting is that the more they are held, the more open people become and the more you, as a manager, will achieve.

After the Meeting

▶ Decide on a specific topic that people will benefit from hearing about or discussing and set a date for the next meeting. Quarterly meetings can be very effective, as long as they take place. If meetings of this nature are consistently cancelled, it will do your reputation more harm than good.

▶ Make sure that everyone who has attended the meeting gets a copy of the action list – the basis of the next meeting's agenda.

▶ Decide who will organise the next briefing meeting.

This briefing approach is great for cross-divisional, departmental and team communication. For example, someone from sales can be asked to do a presentation on a new client, or a new departmental head can be asked to introduce himself and his objectives. It encourages two-way communication and, when done on a regular basis, improves working relationships.

▸ Calling a Meeting to Give Difficult or Bad News

A major challenge for management is always, 'What do we communicate, when and how?' particularly when the news is not so good. The larger the team, the more challenging it is to ensure that the method of relaying news of this type is to the point: short and sweet, but not curt and abrupt. It is also essential for your personality to come through, and that can be difficult when you are delivering a company message with which you do not wholeheartedly agree. This can be when your problems start.

You've toed the company line and held a meeting to tell everyone what is happening, so why is morale so low, and why (you've heard on the grapevine) do people think you know more than you are 'letting on'? Why? Because your body language was at odds with the message you delivered. You felt uncomfortable saying something you didn't agree with, and you didn't actually say, 'I feel uncomfortable saying this. However, this is what will happen …', or 'I find this difficult and believe many of you will find it hard to accept.'

Saying how you feel – in an appropriate way – shows strength of character, and people admire that. There is no need to feel you are being disloyal or that you are divulging more information than you should. If the message is difficult to express, say so. Be honest and brief.

▸ Facilitating a Meeting

To me facilitating is another word for managing, but in a less formal way than chairing. A facilitated meeting is one where a manager encourages creativity by inviting people to be spontaneous and to share ideas. It is a useful method for managers to adopt, especially when planning a new project, gathering ideas or needing to know current issues and concerns. However, facilitating a group meeting can sometimes be likened to putting yourself into a lion's den. The following tips should enable you to thwart such danger.

With the infamous flipchart as your sturdy companion, you will be able to record ideas at source. I prefer a flipchart to a white board for brainstorming or facilitated meetings, as you can keep the flipchart paper for using at a follow-up session if necessary, but more importantly, as a manager it enables you to delegate typing up the information and actions! The additional benefits of using a flipchart at a meeting are:

▸ It helps to focus the group of people at the meeting.

▸ It encourages more active participation from the group.

▸ Ideas are instantly shared as they are recorded in an open meeting and you prevent an information-is-power syndrome developing.

▸ People leave the meeting able to see what has been achieved and knowing what they need to do, when they need to do it, and that is always a good result.

The Role of Facilitator

Keep the meeting or group of people to a number that allows everyone to participate actively: ten is a good number.

Working with large groups

If you are facilitating large groups of people (for example 36) get them to work at round tables in groups of 6. You can then move between tables easily, and once people have completed tasks, a member from each table can feed back to the whole group. You can collate the information at the end of the session. This is much easier than trying to drag information from 20 people or trying to stop a dominating 16 from overpowering the session.

Using the right venue

Make sure the room is large enough to work in, particularly if you are working with a large group. You really need to be able to make good eye contact with everyone in the room. Check the room you will be working in for yourself. I made a really big error recently by agreeing to facilitate a session in a room I was told would be large enough, but when I arrived I found it really wasn't suitable. It was too late to rearrange the meeting, so I started the session feeling uncomfortable and found it very hard to see everyone I was working with. Not good, but a lesson well learnt.

Having a goal

Structure is important, but don't be too rigid. Just don't be over-ambitious with what you want to achieve within a certain timescale. Flexibility is important when facilitating, as long as you maintain a focus on what the outcome needs to be. Even if that is, 'We need three actions to come from this session,' or ' We have to air the current issues and concerns in the next hour,' you have a goal to aim for.

Gaining feedback

It is important to gain feedback, so ask questions starting with what, why, when, where, who or how to ensure people give you information. Asking, 'What gave you that idea?' (known as an open question) will give a far more informative and productive response than, 'Did that idea just occur to you?' (known as a closed question), to which the response can well be a short and sharp yes or no.

Observing the group

You need to be watching a group constantly when you are facilitating – not in an accusative or analytical fashion, but in a manner that encourages people to speak. Recognising body-language signals for positive and negative traits is essential.

I recall working with a group of experienced managers, one of whom thought that the whole exercise we were embarking on wasn't quite what he thought we should be doing. He hadn't said a thing, but his whole demeanour told a very disinterested tale. The biggest giveaway came when he actually tried to hide behind another colleague.

People like this can be really disruptive because they try to turn a group to their way of thinking, little realising that they are actually projecting a very immature and negative image. If you spot this type of behaviour, try to engage the person in conversation to turn their attitude to a more favourable manner, and if this doesn't work – and sometimes it doesn't – it is best to ignore the 'sulking Sam or Sue' and concentrate on the rest of the group to gain a productive outcome.

Maintaining the flow

Very often facilitated sessions are used to gain ideas or to produce better policies and procedures. And some of the ideas people express can be somewhat surprising, in fact off the wall. Overreaction by the facilitator at a time like this can dampen the entire meeting, so a quick 'Mmm' may be best and, if you are the person writing on the flipchart, record the comment and quickly move on. It is better to express your opinion at discussion time than to stop a flow of ideas at brainstorming stage.

Dealing with criticism

Oh yes, criticism: you can be subjected to a lot of that when you facilitate – justified and otherwise. You aren't always going to get it right, and admitting you are wrong is a strength. Facilitating isn't about telling others what to do. You are there to encourage and appreciate another's point of view. Not everyone will agree with you, so don't take the criticism too personally. It's a hard fact of life to live with, but some people seem to enjoy criticising others just for the sheer heck of it. Sad people. If you maintain a friendly and controlling – but not dominating – approach, most people will respond well.

Referring backwards

If you are facilitating a meeting or group session that is covering a number of topics, do refer to ideas and contributions made earlier and tie them into the current discussion. It shows that you have been listening and appreciating the content of the discussion. Suggestions and examples of previous personal experiences, when appropriate, show strong facilitation ability.

Taking a break

If people are becoming bogged down in discussion or are beginning to look weary, a coffee/tea/water break, fresh air, or the odd biscuit or Danish pastry will bring them back on track pretty quickly.

Taking time to think

Give people time to think. It's so easy to expect someone to be talking all of the time. Silence isn't a bad thing – just check that it doesn't go on for too long and that people haven't nodded off.

Being a good listener

Listen. Concentrating on what people are saying and how they say it is the key to being a strong facilitator. You are then able to acknowledge ideas and appreciate good suggestions in a way that will encourage people to give specific examples and evidence of why they believe an idea or suggestion will work. A main aim of facilitation is to assist the progression of ideas, not to encourage a list of ambiguous statements.

Tieing up the meeting

No facilitated meeting or group session should finish without people knowing who is responsible for what action and when the action needs to be completed. A follow-up meeting date should also be agreed before everyone heads for the door.

▶ Using an Interpreter at Meetings

When English is our first language and others do us the honour of speaking our language so well, we sometimes forget that there may be occasions when, because we do not speak the language of a client or foreign colleague, the use of an interpreter would show courtesy and in many instances be more productive. How many of you have sat at global reviews struggling to interpret and understand a foreign colleague because you couldn't speak their language and your company dictated that English was the language to be used? Interpreters can be expensive, but are worth every penny because everyone fully understands one another.

If you do choose to use an interpreter, here are some dos and don'ts to guide you through the experience.

CHECKLIST FOR USING AN INTERPRETER

Do	Don't
Request an interpreter who knows your field of expertise and business.	Assume that because an interpreter understands English and the language of your client or colleague they are automatically able to translate technical terminology.
Brief your interpreter well in advance and try to be idiom free.	Believe that every idiom or colloquialism will be translatable.
Be clear and use short sentences and remember to pause for translation.	Worry if the interpreter takes half the time or twice as long as you do to say something. They may be more concise or be explaining more fully in order for the audience to understand your point.
Address your audience, not the interpreter.	Interrupt the interpreter when they are talking or listening.

Here is a story that illustrates how the use of idioms can get you into trouble. A great friend and colleague of mine and I were addressing an international conference in Prague. We had an interpreter. We were doing a double act, working together well, when there was a need to explain 'gut feeling' and my friend said, 'You know when you feel something in your stomach? You get a feeling that something is good or not so good. You feel it *in your water*.'

The interpreter was fine until she reached the last sentence, 'I do not understand what you mean,' she said. We tried to explain without success. Needless to say, the ensuing laughter from us both was quite infectious and, fortunately, when we could quietly explain exactly what water we were talking about, our interpreter laughed as well. That could have been a really difficult situation and the interpreter could have been one of our greatest challenges. Not so – we were lucky on that occasion.

How many of you have a person you work with who makes your day difficult or the lives of colleagues really unpleasant? You need to be able to interact with 'difficult' people at meetings and in other situations in the workplace. Dealing with such people presents a special challenge, and it's the subject of the next chapter.

CHAPTER 9

Dealing with Challenging People

Sometimes it is hard to explain to other people what it is about somebody that we find difficult and why something that appears petty to another really eats into us. You will probably have an example of your own difficult person, and many of you will have dealt with more than one in your career. You can be sure that there will always be someone who is a challenge to you and for you, and if you are to communicate well at all levels in business and socially, you need to be able to handle the people challenge to the very best of your ability. It's easy to say, 'It's their problem.' It is more difficult but well worth overcoming feelings of frustration, anger and hurt to build relationships with people who behave differently from you.

So often the source of dealing with a challenging person relates to your expectations not being met. You have a set of values and beliefs that you think work well for you. It's when you work with someone who does not have the same set of values or beliefs *and you are unprepared for it* that the problems begin.

I believe there are two main points to remember when working with another person, challenging or otherwise, and they are:

1. Build empathy, and

2. Listen

Sounds soooooo easy, but very often it is soooooo difficult.

When you build empathy with another, you put yourself 'into their shoes'. You don't measure them against what you believe they should or should not be or do, but you accept the person for who and what they are. Often a person we find challenging is someone who doesn't agree with us or our way of working. This is not always the case, but if you just think for a moment about the people who have made your life difficult in the workplace, you may find a common thread, and perhaps, if you are really honest with yourself, that thread is your inability to handle the person.

We are all different: all influenced by different people and situations, upbringing, levels of education, travel and attitude. And all of that has to have an effect on how we work with others. You are unique; every day you will be influenced by others and your surroundings. If a person is positive, happy to deal with change and, although not always agreeing with your every word, able to find a solution to an issue, you pick up the vibes and the atmosphere is healthy and good. You will probably achieve a great deal from working with such a person.

By the same token, if someone is negative, always complaining or finding something to criticise, you often feel weighed down by them and will probably find yourself trying to avoid them or snapping at them. Unhealthy, and not so good.

We can't all be positive all of the time and most of us need to have an opportunity to moan about something or someone. We aren't objects that fit into boxes; as people we are complex: we can be happy and bright one minute and, depending upon how a meeting or conversation has progressed, quite different an hour later. And we are expected to be consistent, willing to help others and able to deal with (constant) change – it's a tall order, isn't it?

When you build empathy with people and listen – really listen – to them, it doesn't matter where you are placed in corporate rankings or the business-experience league; you will nearly always be able to handle a challenging person effectively – I'd say as often as nine times out of ten.

▶ Dealing with Specific Situations

Here are a few colleague-to-colleague challenging situations that some of my clients have identified over the years, with my suggestions on how to deal with them. You'll be pleased to know that 'the challenged' reacted positively and most of 'the situations' were resolved. I have put 'most', as there will always be an occasion when you will need to ask for help in dealing with a person who is making your life difficult – and do make sure you ask for that help just as soon as you realise you need it. Worrying and becoming anxious about something that you can no longer deal with by yourself does not achieve anything. Go to your boss, or if your boss is the problem, to the person responsible for people matters – human resources normally.

People who are Sarcastic

Sarcasm can be very demeaning and puts people down. Many people find sarcasm a good vehicle to hide behind when a difficult situation has to be confronted. To involve a third party and make a sarcastic comment rather than disagree with something is much easier for a person who lacks confidence and the skills to know how to say they disagree in a non-aggressive manner.

Whatever happens, don't feel *you* have to be sarcastic in return. Listen and then ask a direct question in order to sort out any underlying nastiness or problems that may be brewing. Keep calm.

People who are Awkward

People who say something or won't do something just to be awkward can be infuriating. Good questioning techniques combined with helping the person realise that what they say matters can very often lead to them telling you what is *really* bothering them. Again, a lack of confidence very often prevents people saying what the problem is because they feel if they provide a solution, they may be overstepping their lines of authority. If you are a manager, ensure that your people know their boundaries of empowerment for decision making.

People who Change their Minds

People who continuously change their minds over small matters are very often stressed out. They say, 'Yes, I'll attend that meeting for you,' and then at the last moment cancel due to work overload, or they continuously make arrangements or commitments which they don't meet. If you have a colleague who behaves in this manner, a quiet chat away from the hustle and bustle with some suggestions on how they can overcome their time-management problems and a recommendation that they attend a stress-buster workshop will help them and everyone around them.

To change your mind about doing something isn't always a bad thing; in fact, it shows control if you change your mind in order to avert problems that may occur later, but do try not to change your mind every time you agree to something.

The Rotten Apple

To me, the rotten apple is very often a devious politician – someone who would far rather go to someone else and complain or whinge or even discuss better ways of doing something than face up to the person they should tell or confront. This shows a lack of confidence and, very often, low self-esteem because the person who is a rotten apple believes that by using other people, they can never have a finger pointed at them.

Good questioning techniques and an open and honest approach can frequently overcome this problem.

People who Appear Not to Care

These people are very often anxious because they don't feel they know how to do their job properly or they have very low self-esteem. How often do you hear people say, 'I don't care what they think'? Anyone who makes that kind of statement probably cares very much, but because they have experienced being criticised or told what to do in a demeaning manner, they react defensively rather than showing how frightened, hurt or unsure they are. People who appear not to care by doing just what they have to do and no more are also people who need to be asked if they are aware of the way they are perceived by others.

Some people may appear not to care about their career, but not all people are career minded; there are individuals who just want a job that provides money in order for them to do other things. Some people may have a difficult home life and have to fit in a job as well. Others may just need to be told exactly what is required of them and to be asked specific questions if you need to gain information. With many people you have to ask questions continuously, as they don't think to tell you what is happening without being prompted.

People who are Selfish

These people are very often work orientated and focused on exactly what they have to achieve and by when. They prioritise and organise their days and themselves in order to do what they have to do. Great, but they have an irritating habit of not considering anyone or anything else. People who are very 'Me only' thinkers really don't achieve as much as they could.

Point out to these people how much you admire their ability to be focused, but have they considered how others perceive them? Have they considered the benefits of delegating some tasks or listening to others and sharing opinions? By doing so they will achieve more and others will be prepared to help them.

People who are Pompous/Arrogant

The impression given by people who are pompous and/or arrogant is that they are better than you and know more, and they generally demean others. It is usually the tone of voice and not the information that gives this impression. As irritating as it is to deal with, listen to the *content of the message* and comment in a positive manner.

If you work with such a person and have an opportunity to be alone with them, you can point out how you had misunderstood their attitude, and can then comment on what they had to say, telling them how interesting it was and pointing out why you had initially perceived them to be pompous.

People who are Bad Mannered/ Rude/Ignorant

Many people are totally unaware of the impression they make on others. They haven't been taught good manners, their tone of voice alone makes them sound rude, and they do not use considerate words when speaking to people. When the occasion is right, a simple question, 'Why do you find it necessary to be rude to people?' asked not in an aggressive tone but with genuine concern, will often come as quite a shock to them. They will very often say 'I'm not!' To be able to point out how they are perceived acts as a first step to them dealing with the perception.

People who are Small-minded

Some people feel extremely comfortable with their chosen profession or subjects and appear to be very confident. However, as they often lack the confidence in themselves to try new things or to move outside rigid guidelines, they are perceived as being small-minded. Open questioning and good listening can open people up. It is worth trying. Find out whether they are listening to you attentively. If people have made up their minds about what they believe, they will often be concentrating on what they want to say to you and not on what you are saying.

People who Agree with Everything that is Said

Anyone who agrees with everything that is said all of the time is lacking in confidence. They may well be perceived as taking the easy way out, but they often feel that their opinion isn't worthy of being expressed or that they wouldn't be listened to, or they may prefer to do what they are told to do because that way they can't be blamed if they make a mistake or disagree with something. Ask open questions that will enable the person to tell you how they feel, and listen to their answer fully – don't interrupt, and ensure the person knows you value different thoughts from your own.

People with Big Egos

These people show their insecurity. They feel the need to tell everyone constantly what they have done and they must always be the person who people notice. Very often they feel that others aren't capable of doing things as well as they can. Listening and commenting in a positive manner and making people who are egotistical believe you are capable of doing things as well as they can helps to build their confidence in you and makes them able to appreciate that others can do things as well – if differently –

as they can. Again, tactfully asking questions and making such people aware of how they affect others can help. It does depend on how well you know these people, and appropriate timing is very important here.

▶ Getting Help

It's difficult and takes courage to do something when a person is making you feel unhappy. You might almost dread going to work. Make up your mind that you are going to the appropriate person to tell them how you feel and ask for some help. Practise what you are going to say a number of times and if it still doesn't sound quite right, the following format may be helpful. Keep it simple, say how you feel and keep to the facts.

Using the Challenge Format

▶ **Begin by saying how you feel** Upset, angry, frustrated, excluded, bullied, demeaned, intimidated and very unhappy.

▶ **Move on to the situation** Keep to the facts.

▶ **Say what you have done so far** Be clear; say exactly what you have said and how you have behaved. *Do not* get into a 'and then he said this and I said that and what do you think?' dialogue.

▶ **Appeal personally to the person you have approached** 'I need help and believe you are the best person to ask ...'

▶ **Finish with a request for assistance** 'I have tried a number of ways to address this situation and still feel upset. I would really appreciate any suggestions as to how I can resolve this and move on.'

Here is a quick summary outlining the main points to bear in mind when dealing with challenging people.

Checklist for Dealing with Challenging People

Do	Don't
Build empathy and listen.	Prejudge.
Treat each time you meet the person as if it is a first meeting.	Carry forward niggles or resentment from one meeting to the next.
Address issues as soon as possible.	Boil inside until you explode.
Consider your behaviour and how it affects others.	Always blame the other person.
Ask for help if you believe you aren't resolving the challenge.	Believe you have to resolve the challenge by yourself without discussing it with others.
Be clear and concise and use the challenge format when asking for help.	Ramble on and on. Say what you have to say – moan productively and stop.
Be positive.	Be negative.

Who knows what your next challenge will be? You may be lucky today and walk into a challenge-free zone or, on the other hand, you could walk into a complaint: a fellow colleague complaining about the way his boss handled his review, or a customer complaining about your company's poor service. The people challenge has many facets, and being able to complain well and deal with complaints of any nature are two of the important attributes a person needs in business if they are to develop a real sense of business etiquette.

CHAPTER 10

Handling Complaints

So many people shy away from complaining or handling complaints because they believe it is very confrontational, aggressive, loud, dominating and sometimes plain rude. Their experience has probably made them believe that the big 'C' word has all of those meanings. I believe complaining and hearing complaints should be a productive experience for both parties. It's the same old story, I'm afraid: it's what you say and the way you say it that makes a vast difference.

▶ How to Complain

For some people, complaining appears to be second nature – the way they complain leaves a great deal to be desired, but they do complain ... continuously. Complaining productively for most of us is difficult and a skill we haven't acquired because it somehow has a not-nice-to-do feel about it. We tend to hesitate before complaining. Do you find yourself in situations where you know a product isn't quite up to the quality you expect, or a person has behaved in an unprofessional manner, and you um and ah about whether to say something for so long that the moment passes and you feel disgruntled?

The result of this situation is that the product continues to be sub-standard or the person, who may be oblivious to the effect they are having, continues to behave unprofessionally; the company who produced the product has no idea it's sub-standard; and the person who has given the wrong impression of her company will not be given training to help her behave differently. All this negativity continues because you haven't complained.

I can recall an occasion when I bought expensive tickets for a show at a London theatre. It was our family Christmas treat. My girls and I love the theatre and on this occasion my husband – who would much prefer to watch an action film – came too. Good seats? Yes, until the curtain went up. The main part of the action took place on scaffolding so high up that we all had practically to lie down for the performance to see what was going on.

You can imagine the mutterings from my husband and the huffs and puffs as we all wriggled ourselves into the best viewing position. Disappointed? Yes, we were. I wrote to the theatre stating exactly what had happened and how disappointed we were. No angry words, no accusations. We received a refund. The theatre was made aware of our discomfort and disappointment and we received compensation.

If I hadn't complained, my frustration would have made me feel very cheated and the theatre would never have known that expensive seats in row L were useless for that particular show. Complaining productively should result in both parties concluding a difficult situation and feeling OK.

Here is a checklist to help you complain well when you are unhappy with an unacceptable service or product.

CHECKLIST FOR COMPLAINING EFFECTIVELY

Do	Don't
Focus on the facts about the poor level of service or the defunct product.	Attack the person you are complaining to.
Be calm, clear and polite when stating your case, verbally or in writing.	Be aggressive or use threatening language.
Say you are disappointed with the service or product.	Be subjective in your approach and begin listing minute details and the supplier's failings – you won't be taken seriously.
Follow up any verbal complaint in writing.	Forget to ask for the name of the person you are speaking to if you complain over the telephone.
Remember to thank the person who resolves the complaint.	Say what you believe you should receive as recompense before you've fully explained the situation.

Also don't think that complaining in a restaurant is rude, or that it means you are being difficult. When you are subjected to poor service – if, for example, the food you have ordered is cold or inedible when it arrives – call a waiter and *discreetly* complain. It will be appreciated. It's when people are loud and accusatory in their manner that complaints in restaurants are definitely not appreciated.

I must just tell you about a time when I was lunching with the managing director of a large engineering company. We had been working together on a long-term project and needed to finalise some details, so he suggested lunch at a highly reputable establishment, renowned for its delicious food. We were shown to a table from which we looked out over wonderful views. The restaurant was very busy. We ordered our meal. It arrived, beautifully garnished with pansies on the side of the plate. Suddenly, my flowers started to move … and so did his – the pansies were alive with greenfly!

As you would expect, my host complained very discreetly. The other diners must have wondered what had happened when in succession the manager, chef and owner came to speak to us and to apologise profusely. We didn't eat that day, but the champagne went down well.

Handling complaints if a win-win outcome is to be achieved is another skill. Many of you will feel I am stating the (very) obvious when I say a person who complains is unhappy. How often is that person made to feel they are an inconvenience and treated not as an unhappy person, but as a nuisance? All too often, I can assure you.

▶ How to Deal with Complaints

There are three ways by which you can receive complaints: via the telephone, in writing or face to face. In all cases a complaint should be handled as a priority – not pushed to the bottom of your 'to do' pile because it's going to take some time to follow through.

Here are some business etiquette (BE) tips for defusing complaints you receive via the telephone, in writing and in face-to-face situations.

By Telephone

1. Listen fully to the complaint – do not be tempted to overtalk or interrupt the person who is complaining.

2. Give the person your full attention – don't think you can listen and read something else at the same time. You will give the impression that you are uninterested.

3. Politely ask questions to affirm your understanding of the complaint. Do not make the person feel as if they should not have complained or that they are just a number.

4. Ensure the person knows their complaint is being taken seriously and that you will do something constructive about it within a given timescale. 'Mrs O'Sullivan, I will be back to you by 11.15 to let you know exactly what's happening' sounds more reassuring than, 'Mrs O'Sullivan, I will call you by lunchtime.'

5. If you say you will ring – do.

6. If you cannot personally handle the complaint, fully brief the person who will, and get back to the complainer to let them know what is happening and why you have passed the complaint to another person.

7. Ensure that the complainer is satisfied with the resolution and that the unhappy person is now a happy one.

In Writing

1. Read the letter carefully, highlighting the main points.

2. If you have any doubts about your ability to reply to the complaint, speak to your boss. Give some thought to the complaint and go to your boss with suggestions as to how the complaint could be handled. Don't just expect to hand over the whole problem for them to sort out.

3. Respond in a factual and professional manner within 24 hours, clearly stating what you intend to do about the complaint.

4. Always give your full name and telephone number so that the person has a contact.

5. Make sure that what you say will be done is done.

6. Contact the person by telephone once the complaint is resolved to ensure that all is well.

7. Remember that the written word is 'carved in stone'. If you are at all unsure about what you have committed to, have your letter checked by your boss or your legal department, if necessary.

Face to Face

1. Maintain good eye contact while you listen to the complaint.

2. Do not write notes initially. If you listen to what the person is saying, you will retain enough detail to be able to ask meaningful questions.

3. Ask open questions – use Rudyard Kipling's six honest men and true who taught me all I knew; their names were What and Why and When and How and Where and Who – to gain more information. To clarify your understanding of the complaint, use closed questions, beginning your sentences with, 'Do you?' 'Would you?' 'Could you?' in order to gain a yes or no answer.

4. Maintain a pleasant approach – be wary of becoming patronising or being perceived as smirking.

5. Assure the person that their complaint will be taken seriously and say what you will do and by when to resolve the situation.

6. If the complaint is found to be unjustified and has been made without malice, don't smile as if to say, 'You didn't win this time, did you?' A comment such as, 'I'm pleased we

managed to sort that out together' will achieve a win-win outcome and can very often form the basis of a long-term business relationship.

Here are some dos and don'ts to ensure that all the complaints you handle have a positive outcome.

CHECKLIST FOR HANDLING COMPLAINTS EFFECTIVELY

Do	Don't
Treat a complaint as an opportunity to build a better business relationship.	Make the person feel as if they are a nuisance or irritant.
Put a complaint at the top of your 'to do' pile and respond to written complaints within 24 hours.	Procrastinate and leave a complaint before dealing with it – the longer it is left, the more difficult it is to agree a positive outcome.
Listen carefully when you receive a complaint.	Overtalk or interrupt as the person is stating their complaint.
Ask open questions to gain more information and closed questions to gain agreement.	Make a person feel they are being interrogated.
Ask your boss for clarification of what you can or cannot say if you are in any doubt about your ability to handle a complaint.	Commit to something without having the authority to do so.
What you say you will.	Say you will call a person by a certain time and then forget.
Maintain good eye contact in face-to-face situations.	Smirk or patronise.

Do	Don't
Ensure that the complainer is happy with the resolution.	Assume that because actions are taken to resolve a complaint, they will satisfy the complainer.
Give your full name and telephone number so that the complainer has a main contact.	Forget to thank the complainer for bringing poor service or a sub-standard product to your notice.

In any company or organisation, the management team should always be aware of how many complaints are received and how well the complaint is handled. If customer satisfaction is taken seriously in your organisation, you will have a means of tracking complaints. As managers, your ability to support the people working with you and for you when a complaint needs a higher authority shows that every area of communication has been considered in your communication plan and hasn't been left to chance to become yet another topic of gossip for the grapevine groupies.

CHAPTER 11

Five Hot Topics

OK, so now you've reached the juicy bits of this book. They cover a multitude of sins – some hotter than others. I'd like to concentrate on five main topics: I'll start with the lukewarm: punctuality; move on to the smouldering: smoking; carry on to the hotter: rumour, office politics and gossip; work my way through the simmering: gender issues; and finish with the hottest: sex (or not) in the workplace.

▶ Punctuality

Being on time. Many of us will either have a colleague who is an appalling timekeeper or be one ourself. Being regularly late for anything shows a total disregard for others. Yes, there are occasions when, no matter how much time you allow in order to arrive punctually, the unexpected occurs and you are late – that's unfortunate and frustrating and forgivable. But here, I am talking about the person who never ever arrives at work or for an appointment on time, and appears to have a list of the most creative excuses, which they use on a rota basis.

A consistent lack of punctuality shows lack of consideration and is a source of irritation for others.

If You are the Latecomer

If you are a poor timekeeper, do something about arriving on time from now on. You are probably an extremely talented person, who is an achiever and is well respected for your job skills, but if you are always late, people will remember that point about you above all else.

If you cannot manage your time, people will doubt your ability to manage yourself and others. So that next step up a career ladder could be in jeopardy, if you continue to be selfish and disorganised – selfish because you cannot possibly be considering colleagues and the impact your continuous lateness has on them, and disorganised because just how much effort does it take to work out the amount of time you need to be somewhere on time?

Apart from your apparent disregard for others, you aren't being too kind to yourself because you will always be at a disadvantage when you arrive later than you say you will. Hopefully this dos and don'ts list for latecomers will help you overcome your problem, or help a habitually late colleague.

CHECKLIST FOR LATECOMERS

Do	Don't
Calculate the amount of time it takes you to get ready for work and your travel time ... and double it!	Think 'I'll just do this before I leave' – you'll be late.
Allow time for the unexpected.	Get a reputation for being unreliable because of poor timekeeping.
Change your attitude.	Continue to be late.

Do	**Don't**
Set yourself mini-objectives to arrive anywhere on time.	Say you can't change – you can if you want to.
Notice the difference being on time makes to your working day.	Make a big fuss when you do arrive on time.
Take the next step and be five minutes early.	Overreact when comments are made about your new punctuality – a laugh or smile is all that is needed from you.
Recognise the change in attitude of colleagues because you are now punctual.	Try to do too many things when you know you only have enough time to do one if you are to arrive punctually.

Managing Latecomers

And what if you are the manager who has to manage a continuously poor timekeeper? No doubt by now you will have tried every technique you can think of to encourage better timekeeping. Here are a few suggestions; try them – they've worked for others:

Checklist for Managing Latecomers

Do	**Don't**
Address the poor timekeeping issue as soon as it becomes apparent and point out the negative effect it has on team morale.	Talk to other team members about a person's poor timekeeping in a gossipy manner.

Do	Don't
Suggest ways to help the late person manage their time and encourage them to work out for themselves how long it takes them to arrive on time.	Take on all their responsibility by monitoring their every move or being their alarm call – they have to be prepared to improve themselves.
Set the person objectives and ask them to attend meetings at their normal start time.	Make sarcastic comments about lateness and be unrealistic with your improvement timescales.
Give recognition discreetly when the timekeeping improves.	Cheer when the latecomer walks in on time.
Lead by example.	Expect others to be on time if you are always late or delayed.

Setting objectives to encourage a person to be punctual will help them to organise their time. Work with them, encourage them to say what they can do in certain timescales, and always add more time to their timescales and call it 'just in case' time.

▶ Smoking

To smoke or not to smoke, that is the question. It is a personal choice: some of us choose not to, whereas others choose to do so. In recent years, because of research into the pros and cons of smoking, many organisations have opted for a no-smoking policy in their buildings. This means that people who do smoke have to go outside for their nicotine fix or, in some cases, retreat to a smoking room. This recognised workplace practice is covered in the dos and don'ts checklist for smokers on the following page.

CHECKLIST FOR SMOKERS

Do	Don't
Consider the impact you have on others when you are frequently away from your desk to smoke a cigarette.	Take advantage of a cigarette break to gossip for ages.
Appreciate that your cigarette breaks probably add up to a one-hour break per day in total.	Feel disgruntled if your non-smoking colleagues leave the office an hour earlier than you.
Be aware of your manager's attitude to cigarette breaks (particularly if they are a non-smoker).	Be surprised if a manager counts the number of times you go for a cigarette break and then mentions it to you – as far as they are concerned it is non-productive time.
Put on a coat when you go outside in cold weather – I'm always amazed at the various shades of blue people turn in order to smoke.	Litter the entrance of your organisation's building, or that of other company's, with cigarette butts.
Respect a person with definite views on not smoking.	Smoke if you are eating with non-smokers.

A general point here – be aware of how the smell of nicotine clings to clothes, and make sure you aren't remembered for your eau-de-nicotine waft as you walk past people. And for those of you who don't smoke: don't believe that you have to take responsibility for trying to stop a colleague smoking. They know the pros and cons of smoking as well as you do. They have made a different choice from you. To nag a person continuously to give up smoking will have little effect and will only result in making you feel more frustrated. If people do blow smoke all over you, a quiet, 'Excuse me, but your smoke is blowing in my face – could you blow it away from me please?' said in a polite and not huffy or pompous manner normally brings a positive response.

It's hotting up …

▶ Gossip, Rumour and Politics

These have been the mainstay of many a company person's life. Gossips are the people who are *sometimes* unaware of the trouble – yes trouble – they cause. Adding a few more words to a piece of information, without any regard to what is actually said, often changes a harmless statement into a political hot potato. People with the 'gossip and rumour affliction' would do well to take notice of the three wise monkeys: hear no evil, speak no evil and see no evil.

Gossip in moderation can be therapeutic – a great stress reliever. As long as the context is about you and the people you are gossiping with, you are on very safe ground. When you begin gossiping about others, as long as you don't become vindictive, the gossip is still harmless. It's human nature to want to learn something new about others, and sharing information in an informal and chatty manner makes the world go around. It's when people begin to contrive and surmise that gossip turns to rumour-mongering, and that can be vicious and dangerous.

Gossip, rumour and workplace politics generally go together. In business everyone needs to be politically aware. You have to know who is responsible for what and the boundaries of authority. If you don't and you get involved in doing a small piece of everyone's job – without the authority or full set of skills to do so – you and the company would soon be in all sorts of trouble.

It's when gossip, rumour and politics become excessive that people start saying, 'The politics here are a nightmare' or, 'Why can't people do their own jobs and say what they mean to my face

– why do they have to be political and try to score points?' People who find they need to play political games are unsure and insecure. They are poor communicators because they will usually be telling others what they believe they want to hear, rather than what they need to know, and they don't just do it once – they do it with every person who they think will make a difference to their career progression. There are some very rude expressions used to describe such people – I haven't yet managed to find a business etiquette (BE) equivalent – I'll let you know when I do!

I could go on for ever with examples of how people in business build up others and then drop them just as quickly when the devious gossip they've shared doesn't have the desired outcome; or I could tell you tales of people who spend their entire working day finding out the latest gossip in order to feel important. They then believe they know more than others and use the information to trade off with colleagues in order to find out more information of a dubious nature. I'm sure you can identify with my examples and tales and have probably been exposed to similar or the same.

Dealing with Gossip and Rumour

Here is a straightforward checklist to use if you find yourself the subject of gossip or rumour.

CHECKLIST FOR DEALING WITH GOSSIP OR RUMOUR

Do	Don't
Consider how you discovered you are the subject of gossip or rumour: (a) have you sensed it? (b) did a person you trust tell you? or (c) were you told by somebody in a gossipy fashion?	Overreact by marching up to the person who is the number-one suspect for starting the gossip or rumour and challenge them by saying 'I understand you have a problem with me.' It's aggressive and will not produce a positive outcome.

Do	Don't
Talk to the originator of the gossip or rumour as soon as possible.	Use a sharp accusatory tone – stay calm and say how you feel, and tell the person you find it difficult to understand why such gossiping or rumour-mongering is necessary.
Keep your conversation to the point and concentrate on the gossip and rumour surrounding you.	Go off at a tangent and discuss rumours surrounding others.
Focus on a positive outcome.	Shout or dominate the conversation.
Agree with the grapevine groupie what they will do now and say you hope this is the end of the matter.	Threaten or become overly emotional.

If this doesn't work and the gossiping continues, you have to speak to your boss. Stick to the facts – say how you have handled the situation and ask if they can act as a mediator for you and the other person so that both of you can overcome the difficulty and be able to work together.

Dealing with Workplace Politics

If I covered every variation of company or organisational politics, I'd be writing for years. Devious politicking is unpleasant, dangerous and unnecessary. It is detrimental to achieving overall success and a positive working atmosphere, and yet we still need to be able to handle such situations. Here is a dos and don'ts formula for dealing with workplace politics:

CHECKLIST FOR DEALING WITH OFFICE POLITICS

Do	Don't
Be open and honest, say how you feel and stick to facts.	Embellish a story for effect.
Be loyal to people.	Drop somebody just because their face doesn't fit.
Your job professionally and always be as positive as you can be.	Expect to be rated as an achiever if you don't work productively.
Voice your opinion clearly and ensure that people know it is your opinion.	Pass on your opinion as if it is fact.
Have a clear idea of what you need to do to achieve your career goals. Be responsible for achieving your own success.	Believe that simply having a successful person as a mentor will automatically make you rise through the ranks.
Recognise other people's successes.	Envy others' successes.
Acknowledge other people's ideas.	Use another person's idea and claim it as your own.
Speak well of people.	Continuously criticise or find fault in others.

Dealing with Gossip and Rumour as a Manager

Managers really do have to be a Jack (or Jill) of all trades and master of some. Gossip and rumours produced from a healthy grapevine are such an accepted part of the workplace that you can fall into the trap of believing that when you learn what's going on in the company via the grapevine there isn't much wrong with the company's communication. Not so. Information gained from a grapevine can only be categorised as gossip or rumour. That should make it easy to manage. Not so.

If management do not communicate well to the people working for them, then gossip and rumour will be rife, affecting morale and productivity. Gossiping and rumour-mongering take up a good deal of a workforce's time. People need to know what is going on and how they will be affected by any change, and if there isn't a communication process, as a manager, you will have to be dealing continuously with the consequences. If gossip or rumour-mongering is an issue or becomes one for you, try some of these suggestions:

CHECKLIST FOR MANAGING GOSSIP AND RUMOUR

Do	Don't
Use a communication process to ensure that rumour and gossip related to the workplace are kept to a minimum.	Rely on the grapevine groupies to do your job for you – they won't get it right.
Be aware of rumours in the early stages and ensure that any untruths are eliminated.	Encourage rumours by staying silent or by grinning if you are asked a question about a confidential matter.
Get involved and deal with unjustified and malicious gossip.	Allow malicious gossip to be treated as a joke, particularly when it is directed at an individual.
Encourage gossip, rumours and political hot potatoes to be discussed at team meetings.	Ignore or 'squash' people who address difficult issues.

Do	Don't
Accept that you won't have all of the answers all of the time.	Try to bluff your way through when you don't know the answer to a question.
Tell your team as much as you can in an honest manner.	Only half-tell a person or team information that is supposedly confidential.
'Walk the talk' – regularly walk through offices or the areas where people work, and talk to them about themselves, working practices and areas for improvement. You'll be surprised what you learn.	Expect to know your people or learn what is happening at grass roots level if you stay in your office or area of work and only move when you attend meetings.
Encourage a relaxed and open atmosphere in the workplace.	Be a scheming politician if you expect people who work for you to trust and support you.
Show you appreciate people's ability to deal positively with rumours and negative gossip.	Be a 'high-level' grapevine groupie.

▶ Gender Issues

The workplace is a minefield of 'unexploded' issues, and one issue that is discussed more often than most is gender.

I was discussing gender issues with a male colleague, Connor, recently. He currently has a female boss. 'So tell me how you feel about working for a woman,' I asked. The fuse was lit – the issue exploded. I listened to a tirade that went like this:

▶ Why does she think I need advice?

▶ She's challenging my authority.

▶ I've been here so much longer.

▶ I think she's trying to show me up.

▶ She is unfair to criticise.

After listening, I showed him the list and said, 'Now tell me how you feel … and you need to know that she is saying very similar things about you.'

This conversation really made me realise how most of the issues expressed were nothing to do with the fact that Connor's boss was a woman. (I've known him a long time and recalled how he had difficulty building relationships in his last department … and that was all male!) It was all to do with his insecurity. His career had been a bit bumpy and he was beginning to realise that younger, brighter people were overtaking him. He didn't want to accept this and hated to be thought of as a failure – hence the tirade about his boss. His boss was a young, dynamic woman, who was highly thought of and keen to prove herself in a predominantly male environment. When I spoke to her, she listed virtually the same issues as had Connor:

▶ He is challenging my authority.

▶ I think he's trying to show me up.

▶ He is so unfair in his criticism.

▶ Why does he think he knows more just because he has been here longer?

Interesting, isn't it? It has nothing at all to do with gender issues – but everything to do with insecurity and wanting to win or to be better than the other.

Of course, men and women think differently. So does each man you meet think differently and each woman you meet think differently? You have to develop your people skills continuously to deal with the most challenging of situations. If only people who are labelled 'chauvinist' or 'feminist' realised that an aggressive 'I need to be better than him or her at all costs' attitude achieves very little. If you fall into aggressive traps, try thinking differently. The following tips should help you to build better working relationships:

Checklist for Overcoming Gender Issues

Do	Don't
Treat everyone in the workplace, whatever their gender, as colleagues.	Treat people as a male colleague or as female colleague.
Build empathy with everyone – each person will be different.	Treat everyone the same.
Share information and accept advice graciously.	Believe that information is power and that sharing it threatens your authority.
Speak to people in a friendly, professional manner.	Use a bullying, demeaning, hostile, patronising, sarcastic or supercilious tone.
Be open to criticism and remember that if someone is dismissive and demeaning when criticising you, they have the problem, not you.	Criticise in an attacking manner. Beginning sentences with, 'You're wrong' makes you sound very dismissive and small-minded. Far better to acknowledge an idea and add, 'Have you also thought of …?'
Be generous in giving credit where credit is due.	Ask for suggestions to solve a problem and when a person gives you an idea, say, 'That's just what I was thinking of doing!'

Do	Don't
Work with differences.	Believe that men are better than women or that women are better than men.

Working together, respecting differences and capitalising on each other's skill sets ensure the very best kind of teamworking, whether you work in a team made up of men and women, all women or all men. Perhaps many of you are stuck in a time warp and find it difficult to accept the changes that you need to make. Just try using some of the suggestions for overcoming gender issues – you will be pleasantly surprised at how an open-minded approach improves your working day.

Now let's move on to the hottest topic of all.

▶ Sex in the Workplace

Many people meet their partner at work. Nobody can really explain what attracts one person to another – it happens, hourly I suspect. It's great meeting a person you really enjoy being with and who shares similar interests, and when the chemistry also swings into action, there's nothing better.

Romances in the workplace do have their drawbacks because a close relationship between two people – particularly if one is senior to the other – can create resentment and jealousy among everyone else. It can also lead to accusations of favouritism.

If you meet the love of your life at work, be discreet and avoid showing the entire workforce how much you mean to one another until you are away from work. Clandestine meetings in corridors at every given opportunity might be exciting for you, but for colleagues such behaviour can be pretty embarrassing and irritating.

There are occasions when the dangerous liaison becomes a long-term relationship, and that's great. However, this is the exception rather than the rule. Therefore consider the following points if you are thinking about having, or are in, a 'dangerous liaison'.

Don't

▸ Flaunt your affair in front of colleagues – they won't appreciate aside-whispered conversations.

▸ Let the affair take priority over your job – it often does.

▸ Exchange sultry glances across meeting tables – heat spreads and it's noticed.

▸ Allow the emotional ups and downs caused by your affair to affect the way you deal with colleagues.

▸ Continuously discuss your affair with people in the workplace – if you are bursting for a confidante, make it a *true* friend or colleague and make sure any discussion takes place out of work.

▸ Seek sympathy or inflict your pain on others when things go wrong.

▸ Fall into a naivety trap and believe that if your affair ends in an acrimonious way you will be able to continue working well together.

Be wary of beginning an affair at work. You very quickly become the butt of jokes, and no matter how talented you are there are those who will readily talk about your affair and conveniently choose to forget to talk about your achievements in the workplace.

You will appreciate by now that BE is not a prescriptive methodology for handling any situation that you may need to deal with in your working day. My aim is to give you some ideas and suggestions to try so that your personal skills continue to develop alongside your job skills. This chapter has dealt with some areas that have a social connotation, but now I'm moving on to conferences, exhibitions and trade fairs, all of which are hard work and require excellent people skills if you are to gain the maximum value from them.

CHAPTER 12

Conferences, Exhibitions and Trade Fairs

Organisations can reap great rewards from attending conferences, exhibitions and trade fairs. If you are your organisation's representative, you need to be prepared and trained (or well briefed) to gain maximum value for yourself and the organisation from your temporary workplace.

Events of this type have a great buzz about them, and as you are usually meeting and working with people from the same industry or public sector, they give you an opportunity to build better *business* relationships with colleagues and customers. You will notice the emphasis on *business*. Yes, these events are fun, but don't be fooled into believing they are just an excuse to drink, eat and party to excess – you need to be productive in order to give your organisation a significant return on the investment it has made.

Conferences, exhibitions and trade fairs can become dens of iniquity. Most people will be staying away from home and will relax together in the evenings … it's at this stage of the proceedings that you need to consider your professional and personal reputation. It takes years to build a good reputation and ten seconds to ruin it. I've poured many a successful person into a lift before they've tipped beer down the chairman's 'piece of Armani' or gone over the top with sexual innuendos.

I'm not saying don't party; just leave the big one until the last evening. Hangovers the next day aren't a pretty sight and the smell of drink on your breath doesn't encourage a potential customer to discuss your product or service with you, and that, after all, is the main objective of being at such an event – to gain more business.

▶ Presenting a Good Front

Organising conferences, exhibitions and trade fairs is a mammoth task. The people who do it well make it look so simple that almost everyone believes they could be a successful conference organiser. This is not the case, believe me. People who organise events of any kind have special talents and an eye for detail that many with other skills don't even consider, but those details make the difference between an average and excellent event.

There is no way I am going to prescribe how an event should be run, but from the business etiquette (BE) viewpoint, you do need to be aware of the impact you and your company have on customers. If, for example, you are attending an exhibition or trade fair, the stand should always look tidy – there is nothing more off-putting than empty coffee cups or half-read newspapers strewn around a stand. If you are the person in charge of literature, make sure it is on display and that you know where the back-up stock is; rummaging through boxes to find a particular brochure to give a customer doesn't present a professional image or give the customer a good impression.

Welcoming a customer to a stand isn't just about having a good product or a first-class stand design; it is also about having stand personnel who are well informed about the product and have a warm and welcoming manner – even at the end of the day when the pain is creeping up their back and their facial muscles feel stiff from smiling. Personnel at the stand should try to avoid walking towards a prospective customer and asking, 'Can I help you?' Nine times out of ten the customer will make some excuse to move away. People need to be engaged in conversation quickly so a smile and 'open questions' are essential in initiating conversations with prospective customers. Give some thought as to how conversations can begin with potential customers in a way that is natural and comfortable. Here are some possible opening questions; give them a try:

▶ 'What do you think of our stand/new product, sir/madam?'

▶ 'What particular products are of most interest to you?'

▶ 'What do you think of the show this year?'

Remember that it's important to be gracious when a grunt or an offhand remark is received – not everyone will have read this book.

Here is a checklist to aid people who are organising an event for the first time. It could also be useful if you are a manager briefing an organiser.

CHECKLIST FOR ORGANISING AN EVENT

Do	Don't
Set out clear objectives so that everyone attending the event knows what is expected of them.	Assume that representatives from your organisation will automatically know what to do.
Tell people what they are expected to wear at the event, and advise them of the accepted dress for the evening if you are eating out as a group.	Leave dress code to chance – you might get a nasty shock!

Do

Ensure your organisation's representatives and event organisers have the same briefing pack, which includes: layout of venue and stand, stand rules (for exhibitions and trade fairs), 'manning' rota and name of stand manager, product information, emergency contact details and IT support details.

Ensure that all people attending a conference have a complete schedule of events and presentations.

Brief people daily before the event opens to give them information about the previous day's successes and to address any issues that may have arisen.

Implement a lead system to track the business potential.

Expect people to be on stand duty for a maximum of only two hours at a time – people need to look fresh and bright, not tired and wilting.

Organise partner programmes, if your representatives' partners are invited to a conference. As hosts, you should consider their needs as well as those of your employees.

Don't

Choose individuals to represent your organisation at the event who have no product knowledge or who lack the ability to recognise a potential business opportunity.

Forget to put estimated timings on schedules – it is important for people to know where they should be and by when.

Expect people to be at a daily briefing session unless you make it clear that attending is an essential part of the working day.

Lose sight of the reason why you attend exhibitions, trade fairs and conferences.

Expect people to still be smiling sincerely and engaging in good conversation with potential customers if they haven't had regular breaks.

Insist on partners attending events – some people prefer to keep their home lives and business lives separate.

Do	Don't
Always encourage the people from your company to thank everyone involved in making the event a success.	Forget to write a personal note of thanks from your company to the organisers and any external company that has been involved in the event.

There are some practical points to consider when you are working at a conference, exhibition or trade fair:

PRACTICALITIES CHECKLIST

Do	Don't
Make sure you pack two pairs of shoes, ladies, of varying heel heights.	Stagger around in extremely high-heeled, uncomfortable shoes – the pain will show on your face and you will appear disinterested when people speak to you.
Take foot spray with you – it works through socks, tights and stockings.	Forget the plasters just in case you get a blister.
Arrive early in the morning for the stand briefing.	Slide in half an hour after the event has opened and not expect to be noticed.
Be polite.	Show boredom or lack of interest.

▶ Speaking at a Conference

The following are a few pointers for those of you who may be asked to speak at a conference:

▶ Do not drink alcohol. You may think it will calm your nerves, but it won't, and certainly don't drink any type of sparkling drink. I was once at a conference when the speaker, who was drinking sparkling mineral water, opened his mouth to speak … no words, but an enormous burp came forth. I've never forgotten it – a lesson learnt at another's expense, but well worth remembering.

▶ If you are using Autocue, make sure it is adjusted to the correct height for you. I was speaking at a conference once and because the speakers before and after me were six footers, I spent a very uncomfortable 15 minutes with my chin in the air. This was not good because I had no eye contact with my audience, except when I relaxed my neck muscles, and with my chin stuck in the air I gave the impression that I was looking down my nose at them. Always take a hard copy of your speech with you just in case the Autocue goes down.

▶ Always breathe deeply. It is so easy not to, especially when you are nervous. I recall a situation when a colleague of mine (a really good presenter) was waiting for his cue – all of a sudden he turned a deathly shade of pale and rushed from the stage. He had been breathing so shallowly and quickly that he hyperventilated. He regained his composure, returned to the stage and received loud applause for his recovery as well as his great presentation.

SPEAKER'S CHECKLIST

Do	Don't
Drink still water.	Drink alcohol or fizzy drinks.
Breathe deeply.	Breathe shallowly, in short bursts, and hyperventilate.

Do	Don't
Take a hard copy of your speech with you, just in case.	Be flummoxed if the electronic equipment fails; use the hard copy.
Rehearse and be prepared for the unexpected.	Be totally unprepared and expect to be able to improvise, unless you present every day of your life and are confident enough to deliver a speech with little preparation.
Maintain good eye contact with your audience.	Look down continuously, if you are reading from notes.
Smile at your audience unless you are delivering exceptionally difficult news.	Forget to pause for effect.
Be clear and concise and pronounce the ends of your words.	Mumble or race through your presentation.
Stand in a relaxed manner.	Slouch or fidget.

Take advantage of the atmosphere at a conference, exhibition or trade fair to meet and greet as many new people and old acquaintances as possible. Always set yourself goals for achieving networking success at these events. To gain three new business cards will add three new people to your ever-widening and important business network. Networking requires the best possible social skills, the subject of the following chapters. Social skills are essential if your business career is to enter the premier league.

CHAPTER 13

Table Manners

It may seem obvious, but knowing how to handle drinking glasses, cutlery and crockery is high up on the list of social skills. The further up the career ladder you go, the more likely you are to entertain customers, associates and senior colleagues, and at some stage during the entertaining process you will eat. A knowledge of how to do anything properly makes you feel more confident, and even with something as quaint as table manners, a proper knowledge gives you greater poise and makes those around you feel comfortable.

I was prompted to begin coaching people on social skills in business years ago when I attended a large corporate dinner. I was sitting next to the company chairman and a director of a large multinational. Opposite us sat a very bright young man, with a great personality – that's the good bit. The meal began. The young man opposite put his elbows on the table, waved his knife and fork around in the air, ate off his knife and spoke with his mouth full, spraying bits all over the place – not a pleasant sight or experience.

When the young man had left the table, the chairman turned to the director and me and said, 'We must do something about that young man's table manners. We can't have him going to dinner with our top customers behaving like that.' The director added 'I think we ought to make our people aware of the importance of table manners. I am really fed up with being at company functions and losing either my bread roll or drink because people don't know that their side plate is always to their left and their glass is to their right.'

Just how many of the people at the corporate function that night knew that their table manners formed part of their business social skills? Not many, if any. If you know the dos and don'ts of table manners you can be confident that your chances of promotion or clinching that big deal may be spoilt at the meeting table but never will be at the dining table. Since that time, I have coached hundreds of people so that they, like you, have no doubts about table manners when they entertain.

▶ Drinking Glasses

Upmarket restaurants may have up to four glasses of various shapes at the top right-hand corner of the place setting. As a general guide:

▶ The large one will be for water.

▶ The small, bowled one with a proportionately long or embellished stem will be for white wine.

▶ A medium-sized or large tasting glass will be for red wine.

▶ A squat or a narrow glass will be for a dessert wine or port.

There may also be a stocky glass – known as a copita – for sherry, which will be served either as an aperitif or with soup.

If champagne is on order, it will be poured into flute-shaped, sometimes chilled, glasses.

Glasses in many establishments are placed in reverse order to the cutlery (*see page 148*); in other words, the nearest glass will be the first one to use. This is not a general rule, as some restaurants place the red and white wine glasses next to one another, then the water glass.

The waiter should alleviate any controversy or confusion simply by filling the relevant glasses with the appropriate drink.

▶ Cutlery

The general rule as to which implement is used for which course is that you start from the outside and work inwards. If you eat every course, it's fail safe. Skipping courses should not confuse matters, as a good waiter will remove the unnecessary cutlery.

Guide to Table Settings

Working from the outside in, places at the table are usually set so that:

▶ The round soup spoon is on the far right of the setting.

▶ On the far left will be a small fork for an alternative or additional starter.

▶ Next on the right may be a butter knife, identifiable by the absence of a matching fork.

▶ The spatula-like fish knife and its fork will be set next.

▶ Inside the fish knife and fork will be the knife and fork for meat – they will normally be the largest.

▶ The dessertspoon and fork will be either inside the meat cutlery or above the setting. In the upper setting, the fork will be under the spoon with the bowl of the spoon facing to the left and the prongs of the fork facing to the right.

Using Cutlery Correctly

▸ The knife handle is held inside the palm, with the thumb below the blade.

▸ The fork, whether used with a knife or spoon, or on its own, is held similarly, with the forefinger just below the bend.

▸ The spoon is held horizontally like a pen, with finger and thumb together.

▸ Sip from the side of the soup spoon; don't put the whole spoon in your mouth.

▸ The tips of the knife and fork should be positioned so that they remain below the handles.

▸ The handles should never rest on the table when held.

▸ When using a fork and spoon for dessert, eat off the spoon.

▸ When chewing, knives and forks should be placed vertically on the sides of the plate (not hooked on the edges) or held hovering low over it, pointed downwards.

▸Managing Difficult Food

Some food may be unfamiliar to you and require approaching in a particular way.

Globe Artichokes

1. Using your hands, pull off the leaves one by one.

2. Dip the broad ends of the leaves in the accompanying sauce.

3. Using your teeth, scrape and (quietly) suck off the flesh from the end.

4. If a side plate has not been provided, stack the debris neatly around the artichoke plate.

5. Remove the remaining thin leaves and inedible furry choke in the centre to reveal the lush artichoke bottom, known as the heart. Eat this with a knife and fork.

Kebabs

1. If the skewer is hot, hold the top with your napkin.

2. Slide the fork prongs onto the skewer just above the first chunk of food.

3. Hold the top steady.

4. Push the fork down gently and steadily.

5. Ease the contents off piece by piece – not in one wild wrench – until they lie in a tidy line on the plate or rice.

Fish

If you choose fish on the bone you should know how to get the flesh of the fish from the main bone without having to suffer the indignity of dealing with a mouthful of bones.

To eat the flesh from a flat fish: firstly, with your fish knife and fork remove the head and tail from the fish and move them away from the remaining flesh. (You can also cut off the small bones around the edge of the fish.) Secondly, with your fork holding the fish, use the tip of your knife to draw a line down the fish's backbone and then scrape the flesh away from the backbone towards the edge of the fish (this avoids picking up a mouthful of bones). Thirdly, turn the fish over to carry out the first and second points all over again: place your knife underneath the fish and your fork on the top and then slowly turn the fish over, turning it away from your body.

If you do not feel comfortable boning a fish – and it does take practice – either avoid choosing fish on the bone when you are entertaining or being entertained, or ask the waiter if the fish could be boned for you; in many good restaurants the waiter will ask you if you would like the fish boned for you, and personally I think it is better to be safe than sorry and take advantage of the offer.

Lobster

This is best eaten using lobster prongs, a bone-cracker, a finger bowl and a large napkin:

1. Use the bone-cracker to open the claw.

2. Use the prongs to poke into parts of the shell that are difficult to reach, and to scoop out the flesh.

Mussels

Ask for a finger bowl if you have not been given one.

1. Use your hands to remove the top shell.

2. Open up the first mussel shell with your fingers and remove the mussel with a fork.

3. You can use the two halves of the empty mussel shell to remove the other mussels cleanly from their shells.

4. Use the shell to scoop up the sauce.

Oysters

1. Pierce the lemon wedge or slice with a fork and squeeze over the oyster and/or add a speck of cayenne pepper.

2. Lift the shell to your mouth with your hand.

3. Gracefully throw back your head.

4. Swallow the oyster whole.

5. Soak up the sauce with brown bread.

The less hearty may prefer to:

1. Use the flat side of an oyster fork to prize the flesh from the shell.

2. Pierce it with the fork prongs.

3. Swallow the oyster whole.

4. Mop up the sauce with brown bread.

Snails

Use special tongs and a small fork.

1. Holding the snail shell between the tongs, twist the snail flesh free of the shells using the fork.

2. Use the fork to dip the snail flesh in sauce and convey it to your mouth.

▶ Adding Condiments to Food

Food that has been well prepared and cooked should have been adequately seasoned, so it is not good manners to season it before you have tasted it. If you feel you need additional seasoning, or if a sauce is offered to accompany the dish, the following guidelines should help:

▶ **Salt** should be placed on the side of the plate. The food should then be conveyed to it on the fork and salt pressed on with the knife.

▸ **Pepper** is ground from a grinder or shaken on.

▸ **Sauces** and **mustard** should be placed on the plate with a separate spoon.

▸Some Basics

It is worth remembering these basic rules for polite and enjoyable eating:

When does the eating start?

The host should ask his guests to begin as soon as their dish has been served. It makes little sense to allow food to get cold.

When is it impolite to lean across someone to reach something?

Always, because it makes the other person feel awkward. Better always to ask the nearest person to the item to pass it over.

When should you apologise for talking to someone across the person next to you?

As soon as you do it. An explanation and an apology should be offered.

What happens if eating implements are dropped on the floor?

Yours or someone else's should be left there and the waiter asked for replacements.

Why are soup bowls tilted backwards and the spoon scooped away from you?

The practical reason is so that any spillage arrives back in the plate and not on the lap.

What's the answer to the perennial pea predicament?

Spear a few peas on the prongs of your fork and press a few more lightly on top. It is acceptable to eat peas on an upturned fork, but you must hold the knife in your right hand to guide them onto the front – not the side – of your fork. Less formally, if it's a fork supper you can use your fork in your right hand.

Should you use a toothpick at the table?

Not unless you are prepared to look ungainly and unsightly. It's not an appetising sight, even when performed behind a napkin or with one's head twisted away. If you must – and some restaurants leave toothpicks on the table – retreat to the ladies or gent's to deal with the offending debris.

How do you choke politely?

If food is caught in your throat and you feel a choking fit coming on, leave quietly and work it out in the ladies or gents.

How does one remove unwanted food from the mouth?

Elegantly turn your head discreetly away from the table and remove it behind your napkin. Leave the fragments in the napkin, place it under your chair and ask for another.

How do you signal that you have finished a dish?

By placing the knife/spoon and the fork together vertically or at twenty past four on the plate.

Under what circumstances may you smoke during the meal?

Never smoke between courses and always ask if you may smoke over coffee. At formal functions, people shouldn't smoke before the Master of Ceremonies announces, 'Ladies and gentlemen, you may now smoke if you wish.'

What about cigars?

As above, but they should also be offered around the table.

When is the meal formally over?

When the host stands and signals that it's time to move on.

Use the following checklist to refresh and refine your table manners where necessary.

TABLE MANNERS CHECKLIST

Do	Don't
Use the side plate to your left for bread and rolls.	Use the side plate to your right … it's not yours.
Break off small portions of a bread roll with your fingers. Spread on a small portion of butter (if you eat it) and put the piece of bread into your mouth.	Worry about the crumbs, or carve up a bread roll with your knife, or spread it thickly with butter and bite into the whole roll.
Break sweet or savoury biscuits into bite-sized pieces.	Dunk a sweet biscuit or cram a whole savoury one into your mouth.
Cut food into small, bite-sized portions; then if you are asked a question as you put something into your mouth, the answer won't be too long in coming.	Speak with your mouth full – no, not even with food in your 'squirrel pouches'.

Do	Don't
Allow yourself time to savour your food.	Race through a meal as if you only have ten minutes during which to eat it.
Transport your food and drink all the way to your mouth via forks, spoons, glasses and cups.	Bend your body forward with your mouth open to meet food and drink halfway.
Place your eating implements down on your plate while speaking – they are for eating only, not for gesticulating to emphasise a point.	Choose difficult-to-eat foods – such as pasta with tomato sauce – when entertaining a client. You can bet your life a blob of tomato will appear somewhere!
Keep your elbows into your sides when eating.	Dig others in the ribs with your elbows or spread your arms out when eating.
Rest your forearms only on the table – and only when there is no food to be eaten.	Lay or put your elbows on the table.

You never know, do you, what people's 'hot buttons' are in business until you get to know them really well. And yet for many of us, our business relationships frequently begin over a meal. So many people have told me that their 'hot button' is table manners and how they have been put off people by their lack of them. I hope you have refreshed your knowledge of table manners or gained some new insights to ensure you don't press that particular 'hot button' in the wrong way with your clients or senior colleagues. Talking of hot buttons, that brings me to a very pleasant subject, wine and drinking.

CHAPTER 14

Wine and Drinking

When you entertain in business, it helps if you know something about wine. When I enjoy a wine, I remember it; I sometimes make a quick note of it in a notebook, as it's a useful way of building a mini-understanding of a vast subject.

If you are entertaining a wine expert, great – take advantage of their expertise and enjoy. My aim here is not to make you an expert overnight; it is simply to give some guidelines.

I do think it's worth mentioning here that many organisations don't encourage long lunches with alcohol, and some don't even allow them. People still lunch, but most execs will drink water at lunchtime; on rare occasions they may drink a glass of wine but usually no more than two. However, the vino does tend to come out in quantity at evening meetings over dinner.

▸ Choosing Wine

Among the sweeping, but safe, advice on choosing wine is:

▸ Red wine with red meats.

▸ White wine with fish and poultry.

▸ Rosé generally as for white, or with light vegetarian, spicy and Oriental dishes.

▸ The fattier the food, the younger (and sharper) the wine.

▸ Match the fullness of the wine to the richness of the food.

Better still, ignore all those generalisations and drink what you really like. For example, a light, fruity red, a crisp rosé or a dry white goes with most foods. .

▸ Ordering Wine

You match the wine to the food, and not normally the other way around, so wine should be selected after people have chosen their food. As the host of a large gathering, you should ask your guests for their wine preferences.

In top traditional restaurants, a wine waiter, or sommelier, is usually identified by a key and/or tasting spoon around his neck. Wine waiters are usually really helpful and only too pleased to recommend or help you decide on the wine most suitable to enhance your meal.

▸ Course-by-course Suggestions

It is worth investing in a wine book that will introduce you to the different wines from around the world and describe their qualities. Although personal preferences override what wine goes with what food, here are some rudimentary guidelines:

Hors d'oeuvres   Crisp, dry and light, fruity.

Soup   Dry for light soups; Madeira for thick soups; crisp, dry white for medium-bodied soups.

Pâté	Light red.
Seafood	Crisp, dry white; dry sparkling. Choose a fuller-bodied wine for seafood with sauces.
White meats	Light, fruity red, or medium-dry/dry white.
Red meat and game	Hearty red.
Oriental and spicy	Dry white or fruity rosé; although personally I always order beer with curry or spicy foods.
Pasta	Light, fruity red. If cream based, choose a dry white.
Vegetarian	Soft or light reds and rosés.
Desserts	Choose wines equal in sweetness.
Cheese	For soft cheeses choose a light, fruity red; a dry, fruity white for medium cheeses; a hearty red for hard cheeses; a fruity red or sweet wine for blue cheeses; an aromatic, crisp, dry white for goat's cheeses.

▶ Tasting Wine

All wine should be brought to you as the host to taste. If it has been chosen by one of your guests, then the guest should taste it.

You will be shown the bottle to examine the label. The bottle must not be open. If it is, it should be firmly refused. Having opened the bottle, a wine waiter may hand the host the cork.

This is to savour the bouquet, as well as to confirm that it has not dried out or is corked (*see below*).

A house wine will not normally be offered for tasting, although you can ask to taste it if you are unfamiliar with the label.

Why Taste Wine?

The purpose of tasting wine is not to find out if you like the flavour. It is to check that the temperature is right and that it is in good condition.

If you order subsequent bottles of that same wine, you should taste each one before it is poured for your guests. This is not essential, but it will enable you to avoid the rare corked bottle.

▶ Serving Temperatures

Red wine is generally drunk at around room temperature (20°C). Among the exceptions are some very young fine red wines, such as Bordeaux, which are chilled; more delicate wines, such as Burgundies, should not be chilled.

White and rosé wines should be chilled and placed in a wine cooler during the meal.

▶ Rejecting Wine

There will be times when you will have to reject a wine after you have tasted it.

Corked Wine

A defiled wine – mainly called corked – is not difficult to detect. Many people say a wine is corked when in fact it's just a poor-quality wine. So err on the cautionary side, as corked wine is very rare. Other than the sensation that you have just sipped from a Victorian swimming pool, its characteristics are:

▸ A vinegary taste that burns the throat.

▸ A brown tinge in a white wine, or a deep brown colour in a red.

▸ The cork smells sharply of sherry.

▸ A musty, mouldy or decaying taste.

▸ No redeeming aroma.

▸ Cloudiness or murkiness.

Cloudy Wine

Cloudy red wine can mean something is wrong. On the other hand, it could be that the sediment in the bottom of the bottle has been disturbed.

If you suspect that a wine is off, but are uncertain, discreetly ask the wine waiter to taste it. He may do so or more probably will take your word for it. Should he disagree, you should politely request another bottle.

▸ Serving Wine

Having tasted a sample of the wine, ask the waiter to serve it to your guests. The waiter should pour it gently, treating it with respect and, if it's a red, doing so without disturbing any sediment.

Glasses should be filled up to two-thirds: the top third is where the bouquet lives. After the guests have been served, the waiter returns to charge your glass.

Although the wine waiter should ensure that no glass remains empty, if you are the host, this is your ultimate responsibility. So if the waiter is otherwise engaged, you should take over. Your guests' glasses should remain on the table and the bottle must be brought to them, even if it means you circum-navigating the table.

If you do not wish the waiter to refill your glass, just say so, or cover your glass with two closed fingers.

▶ Holding Wine Glasses

▶ Glasses containing white and rosé wine and all other chilled wines are held by the stem.

▶ Red wine glasses should be held just under the bowl.

▶ Opening Champagne

Champagne comes from the strictly defined Champagne region in France. Its fizz is the result of secondary fermentation in the bottle.

If you wish to open the bottle yourself, don't use the flamboyant Grand Prix method! Do be aware that a cork in flight is seriously dangerous. For a minimum of wasted foam, an elegant display and a winning pop, do it this way:

▶ Aim the bottle away from the table or people and in a safe direction.

▶ Place the palm of the hand over the cork as you unfasten the wire cage.

▶ Slowly rotate the bottle itself, holding onto the cork and the cage.

▶ Steer into a 45-degree angle and twist the cork off gently while holding it in your palm.

▶ Enjoy.

And to complete the wining and dining experience ...

▶ Choosing and Drinking Cognac and Brandy

Cognac is a high-quality brandy distilled from grapes and produced in the French town of the same name. Everything else is just brandy, which is also produced from other fruits.

Brandy is normally drunk at the end of the meal, along with coffee. To release its bouquet, cup the goblet and gently swirl it until it feels the same temperature as your hand.

WINE AND DRINKING CHECKLIST

Do	Don't
Enjoy!	Overindulge!

I've included a very short checklist for this chapter because when you are entertaining, those are the two most important points for you always to be aware of. We all overindulge on occasions, but if you do so at business functions, you run the risk of developing a loose tongue and losing credibility. However, a tongue isn't the only part of your anatomy that can let you down, is it? Our bodies can be real enemies on occasions and expose us to all sorts of social taboos, which are discussed in the next chapter.

CHAPTER **15**

Social Taboos

Well, what a can of worms this is! How often have you found yourself in an embarrassing situation and really haven't known what to do to hide your confusion? Knowing how to cope with embarrassing situations and common hazards that need to be dealt with at business social functions makes you feel more confident. So let's begin with this permanent enemy of yours and mine.

▶ The Body as an Enemy

We all need to know how to deal with those difficult moments when our body does embarrassing things while we are in company. Although humour often relieves embarrassing situations, don't let it become too raucous or it will add to the embarrassment.

Sneezing

This is not supposed to be a shared experience, so if you feel a sneeze coming on, make sure your hand is halfway to your mouth at the first, tingle-in-the-nose stage, and try your best to have your mouth covered completely and your head turned away by the time you reach the '-shoo' stage. 'Excuse me,' in an apologetic tone completes the happening.

Coughing

Coughing and spluttering, and then a ghastly noise and a 'splut' sound, repulse most people. When you cough, your mouth should be covered and your head turned away from others. If you do have congestion, use a handkerchief ... but please do not observe its contents!

Hiccups

Aren't these horrible things? Said to occur because of tension, they begin at totally the wrong moment: in the middle of a conversation with a new client. All you can do is retreat to the ladies or gents (busy places aren't they?), try some deep breathing and drink some water slowly. Don't forget to excuse yourself before you speed away covered in confusion.

Bad Breath

Yuk! If your innards are functioning well and you visit a dentist regularly, clean your teeth and floss twice a day, this shouldn't affect you. Oh, you had a curry or garlic last night? Well, out with the breath freshener immediately or, of course, you can always carry a pot of parsley around with you – parsley really works, and I'm told sucking tea leaves does as well (although I wouldn't personally fancy that at all).

Yawning

This is another hand-over-the-mouth situation, without too much noise please. If you do feel a yawn coming on, clenching your teeth together stops the rhino look, but the clenched-teeth look can make your face look distorted. A hand over the mouth and a quiet, 'Oh, do excuse me – I didn't sleep well last night' should suffice.

Breaking Wind

If this can be ignored, it should be. Humour should be avoided here, as you run the risk of hysterics breaking out, and no pulling faces or loud comments either. If it happens to you and you can't ignore it, say, 'Excuse me' and if you can walk away, do so!

Rumbling Stomach

It depends where it happens and who you are with. Usually I say, 'Excuse me – it must be nearly a meal time' as my rumbles seem to be indiscreet – but if you can ignore it, do so.

▶ Handling Other Awkward Situations

So now the body enemy is conquered, let's consider how to handle table accidents, bores and drunks.

Handling Table Accidents

I can remember sending a pot of tea flying in a crowded tearoom and feeling mortified because the tea went over at least four people. I grovelled and muttered, 'I'm sorry' at least 25 times, I think – not the right thing to do. If accidents happen at a table – such as food or drink spilling – use a napkin to mop up until the waiter arrives to help. Apologise *once* to your guests and to the waiter and handle the situation with as little disruption as possible.

Controlling Bores

Bores usually come in two categories: the person who talks because he or she is nervous, and the person who has never learned to listen.

One good way of dealing with benign bores is to steer them into dialogue mode by frequent polite interruption and questions. That often helps a nervous bore feel more confident and, eventually, able to ask those three warm little words: 'What about you?'

Going to the ladies/gents is the knee-jerk reaction to brazen bores. But that's risky: if you are of the same sex you could be followed there.

Safer is to locate someone you have to speak to urgently.

Subtler is to apologise for monopolising the bore and suggest you should both circulate more.

Unwise is to introduce them to someone else, because that someone could turn out to be an important business contact who will remember the gesture.

Perilous is to complain that the stuffy atmosphere is getting to you and you need a stroll; they may decide they feel the same.

Submitting is often the only recourse, particularly if the bore is an important client or a company senior. In this case, you can try to cling to consciousness by constantly changing the subject. It works with many bores, because as long as they hear the sound of their own voice, they don't worry too much what it is saying. So don't ever be nervous of interrupting them at reasonable intervals, particularly when you preface your conversation with variations on the theme of, 'I'd be interested to hear your opinion on . . .' The trick is being able to remember what they've already covered.

Dealing with Drunks

A drunk is an embarrassment and a threat, particularly if he or she represents the host company.

If you are at a function for company personnel and you notice a colleague exhibiting:

▶ A slightly raised voice.

▶ Speech speeding up.

▶ Deepening or blotchy complexion.

▶ Physical agitation.

▶ A belligerent tone.

Discreetly guide them out of the room and to a location where, with someone at their side, they can begin to sober up. These relatively benign symptoms can usually be dealt with without fuss.

Dealing with the Seriously Drunk

It is not so easy to deal with someone who has progressed into the classic unfocused-eyes-and-swaying-frame stage. A colleague who is drunk and has got out of control before you can reach them may be surrounded by guests pretending not to notice, but who are actually too embarrassed to deal with them. The mission of the host company representatives is to get the drunk out of there, but at all times:

▶ Resist treating the person like a silly child or a damned nuisance. Instead, be calm in everything you do and say.

▶ Don't patronise or bully. The inebriated are frequently very sensitive to tone and atmosphere and have amazing memories.

▶ Maintain a firm and polite manner. In most situations, this gives you the best chance of cooperation.

▸ Summon whatever assistance is available: preferably a colleague of yours or of the drunk, or a member of the catering staff.

▸ Escort the person from the room.

▸ Settle them in a quiet room with some water and coffee and a guardian.

▸ Allow them to recover some measure of balance.

▸ Even if the person claims to be fully recovered, their reappearance could disconcert other guests, and there will be the continual anxiety that they will plunge back into their earlier state. Get them out of there!

▸ Call a cab or arrange some other transport, and have someone take them home.

Here is a social taboos checklist to help you through embarrassing situations:

SOCIAL TABOOS CHECKLIST

Do	Don't
Use humour to lighten a potentially embarrassing situation.	Let the humour over an embarrassing situation become too raucous or demeaning.
Cover your mouth when you are about to sneeze, cough and, if you are too late to clench your teeth, yawn.	Splutter over everyone, or open your mouth as wide as you can, or make as much noise as you can muster.
Relax and drink water when you get hiccups.	Let the hiccups go on for ages – they'll be really uncomfortable for you and irritate others.

Do	Don't
Get regular dental checks and carry breath fresheners with you.	Breathe over everyone when you've eaten garlic or curry.
Ignore the fact that you or another has broken wind, if you can!	Use humour – you run the risk of hysterics breaking out.
Say, 'Excuse me, it must be close to a meal time,' if your stomach rumbles loudly.	Feel you have to say anything – you can ignore it.
Apologise once and handle the situation with as little disruption as possible, if you spill food or drink at a table.	Continuously apologise and get flustered – you'll make it difficult for those around you.
Recognise ways in which you can control a bore, and always be careful that you aren't encouraging that state in others.	Introduce a bore to someone else because that someone could be an important business contact.
Help a colleague if they are worse for wear through drinking too much.	Leave a colleague to suffer the consequences of being drunk at a company function when you could have helped.

There must be so many business social situations when some of the taboos I've covered here rear their ugly heads. It is easy to believe that a business social occasion is a time to eat, drink and be merry with customers and colleagues. So often, no consideration is given to the fact that such occasions are 'dressed up' business meetings, where opportunities for networking and marketing your organisation abound.

CHAPTER 16

Business Entertaining

You must have business social skills if you are to build strong business relationships and be a prominent player in the premier business league.

Preparation, objectives, ability and follow-up are all main areas of business entertaining which are often overlooked. The social side of business should be an enjoyable and rewarding experience for you and your customers, colleagues and company. Always remember, however, that business entertaining should be kept relevant to business, and that it should not be treated as a leisurely time out with friends; a big trap to fall into is thinking that business entertaining is an excuse to gossip and drink until the legs give way. Whether you are a host or a guest, if you are to gain real value from business entertaining of any kind, it needs to be treated like an important business meeting.

My aim here is to give you some tips on how to achieve successful results from an event of any type. Those who organise events – marketing department staff, the boss's secretary, manager's assistant or outside organisers – work long hours in often difficult circumstances to ensure success. It is therefore necessary for anyone working with these hardworking professionals to know how to complement their efforts by hosting and guesting professionally.

▶ Using a Technique

Some of you will be attending business events or dining with colleagues and clients for the first time, and I'd like to suggest that you use a technique to help you overcome some of your nerves. For newly appointed managers needing to achieve as much business credibility as possible from entertaining, this technique will work for you and your people. It gives you a good tracking method. You and your team set the objectives you want to achieve and after the event, you review them.

The most experienced of you, who entertain and attend business social functions most days or weeks of your life, will probably have developed your own methods to achieve success from such events. Because your methods are second nature to you, you may find it difficult to understand why others in your team or company cannot, perhaps, do the same. This technique might work for them – it will also give you a clear idea of what is being achieved from the numerous business social expenses you sign off.

▶ How To Use the Technique

This technique is built around setting realistic expectations or objectives for achieving success. It ensures that you achieve a result from every business social situation. It is simple and effective.

Most of you will be used to setting goals or objectives in business. Sometimes, when you set only one and don't achieve it, you are disappointed and despondent ... try setting yourself three!

The objectives: Best case

OK case

Worst case

Here are just a few examples of how to use this approach in a business social context. I'll begin with a familiar business social scenario and some sample objectives:

Scenario – Meeting New People

When you attend a business reception and you are the only representative from your company, and you don't know anyone who will be attending, use this technique to encourage you to circulate and meet the 'unknown'.

Objectives

Best case   Meet three people tonight, give a business card to all three, arrange an appointment with one and speak to the other two within the next week.

OK case   Meet two new people, exchange business cards and agree to call one of them to arrange to meet within the next month.

Worst case   Introduce yourself to five people, exchange business cards and agree to call them in the next two weeks. In this instance you will only have introduced yourself to people rather than spending some time with them, and will not have arranged to meet in the near future.

This technique works because if you achieve *any* of the these objectives, you will have achieved more than just turning up at a function and hoping you'll be lucky.

Scenario – Inviting a Business Contact to a Reception

You invite a person to a business reception who you believe will be a useful business contact. She works in the same industry sector as you do, and has a professional reputation and good business contacts. You are both currently working with a client, and there is no conflict of interest as far as the client is concerned, as the products from your contact's company complement the services your consultancy/company offer. Without setting any expectations, you would probably chat quite amicably, talk about industry people and business in general – all good stuff. By using the best, OK and worst-case technique, you will achieve much more.

Here is an example, using the scenario:

Expectations (or objectives)

Best case   To build rapport and discuss a business opportunity that you could both work on. Agree a date for meeting with the client together.

OK case   To build rapport and talk about the possibility of working together in the future. Agree a date to meet again with some identified business opportunities to discuss more fully.

Worst case   To ascertain whether or not there would be any joint business opportunities. If so, arrange to call and make an appointment to meet again in two weeks' time.

In each case, there is a positive outcome: if you come away from the reception only having achieved the worst case, you will still have achieved more than having a cosy chat with no direction, and the guest could also use the technique to equally good effect to achieve results.

This approach may appear 'salesy' to some of you who don't work in that much-maligned profession. It really doesn't matter what profession you work in, you still need to make contacts with people in your own profession and others, and if you do anything with a purpose, it makes you feel and appear more confident. This technique can be used in any business or business social situation to encourage and build confidence and to give you direction when you are placed in a situation that is outside of your comfort zone.

Using the Technique in Different Circumstances

▶ If you are meeting people for the first time, make sure you know something about them and their company, and use that information so that you can ask meaningful questions. Use the technique here to set your objectives and get a new business relationship off to a good start.

▶ For clients you've worked with before, the objectives have to be focused on maintaining and building your relationship. You can utilise information about new services, the client's successes and new opportunities. Use the technique to achieve something from each of these sectors.

▶ If you have recently sealed a contract with a client, your main objectives have to be built around saying 'thank you' and developing your working relationship for the future. Your client also needs to feel comfortable with you, and if you speak and behave purposefully but not aggressively, you will build confidence. Using this simple but effective technique enables you to have direction, but not be pushy.

▶ The Business Meal

Now that you know what you want to achieve, we can move on to one of the most popular forms of business entertaining: the business meal. At best, business lunches and dinners are productive and a pleasure. At worst, they are tedious and time wasting ... and why is that? Because at the outcome of the productive and pleasurable meal you had set some goals – even if you did so subconsciously. However, the tedious and time-wasting meal, where you achieved nothing, was probably the result of no goals being set or you feeling decidedly unsure of yourself. An ability to host well and be the perfect guest are essential social skills for anyone.

Hosting a Business Meal

When you invite a client or colleague to a meal, this is normally done very informally, face to face, by telephone or by e-mail. As host (female or male) your five main responsibilities are to suggest the venue, book the table, make the client feel comfortable, pay and know you've achieved something when you leave the restaurant.

Choosing a restaurant

▶ It's a good idea to build personal and company relationships with a small group of restaurants within various price brackets; the benefits should include a warm and personal welcome for you and your guests, and the service should be that much more pleasant than it could be without such a relationship.

▶ Ask your guest if they have any eating preferences, for example if they are vegetarian, or if they 'can't stand' highly spiced foods or 'love' fish. Ensure in advance that the restaurant you choose can accommodate your guest's tastes.

▶ Restaurants vary considerably and most people enjoy trying the latest 'fads and fancies'. If, however, you don't know your client or colleague well and really don't have the opportunity to discuss their preferences with them, err on the cautionary side and opt for a traditional restaurant with an excellent reputation.

Confirming the appointment

▸ It's a good idea to contact your guest by telephone the day before just to confirm that all is well and that the appointment is still convenient.

Dealing with timing issues

▸ Timing is an essential element of successful entertaining, and if you are meeting a guest at a restaurant, you should always be there to greet them on time – preferably five minutes early.

▸ If your guest is late and you cannot contact them, sit and wait without ordering for 30 minutes. If you know they are travelling some distance or via a notoriously busy motorway, allow another 30 minutes. Then ask the waiter if you can order, and if your guest arrives all of a fluster, calmly state that you have just ordered, get them a drink and ask the waiter if your order could be put on hold until your guest orders.

▸ When your guest arrives and you are exchanging the initial pleasantries, check how long they have for the meal. There is nothing worse than being halfway through something quite delicious and realising that your guest is looking at their watch continuously and beginning to shovel food down at a rate of knots. Being prepared enables you, as host, to make the waiter aware if your time is limited, and for a taxi to be ordered, if necessary, to ensure that your guest makes their next appointment on time.

If your guest doesn't turn up

▸ If you are stood up, a short e-mail or note expressing your disappointment that your guest couldn't keep your appointment, and adding that you hope they are well and that you look forward to speaking to them soon, will help to cover over any embarrassing cracks. It will also give your guest an opportunity to apologise if they have completely forgotten the appointment.

▶ If your guest has forgotten and they ring to apologise, firstly say how pleased you are that they are well, then reiterate your disappointment at not seeing them, and if they sound amenable to rearranging there and then, fix another date … and hope they will remember next time.

The preliminaries

▶ Guests should always be offered the best seat. Avoid the engrossed in conversation, pulling out your own chair, sitting down, elbows on table 'Wow, I'm ready for a drink – how about you?' routine. A simple, 'Where would you prefer to sit?' is much more considerate.

▶ As a host, you should wait until your guest is seated before sitting yourself. If you are a woman and the men refuse to sit until you have, smile and sit rather than playing 'after you'.

Ordering the food

▶ When ordering, you have a choice as host: you can enquire what your guest would like and then order for them, or when the waiter asks for your order say, 'After you' to your guest, so that they can order for themselves. Most people nowadays order themselves, but there are still occasions when a host orders on a guest's behalf.

▶ Waiters will ask women for their orders first; these should be followed by your principal male guest. As host, you are expected to orchestrate who should order next by naming them.

▶ If you have taken your guests to a 'new experience' – a restaurant serving food which you are very familiar with and they are not – then either allow them to browse through the menu and make comments about the tastes and ingredients of certain dishes, or suggest that you order a selection of dishes for them to enable 'the experience' to be tried and tested. Don't forget to warn people if any hot or pungent spices are included in a meal – a client or senior colleague will remember you for the wrong reason if they leave the meal with a burnt mouth.

▸ As host, suggesting the venue for your meal should eliminate any embarrassed expletives when you receive the bill. You should choose a restaurant that you know and that comes within your budget. If your guest chooses the most expensive meal on the menu, try not to look at them in a demeaning manner, and definitely don't make any kind of remark about their choice other than, 'That sounds good, doesn't it? I was tempted myself.' You've asked, you chose, you pay.

Handling restaurant staff

▸ When you need to attract the attention of a waiter or waitress, raise your hand and say, 'Waiter/waitress.' If they don't hear you the first time, use a slightly louder, 'Excuse me.' Do not shout and click your fingers. When you are trying to attract a waiter's or waitress's attention, be conscious of the fact that they can hardly serve you if they are in the middle of serving another table. The best time to catch their eye is when they are moving between tables.

▸ Be attentive to your guest without constantly asking if every-thing is all right. If your guest is dissatisfied with their meal, discuss the problem with them *quietly*, and apologise, excuse yourself from the table and tell the head waiter of your guest's dissatisfaction, or discreetly call the waiter and quietly explain what the problem is. Do not get into a heated discussion. If the problem isn't handled well, and in my experience that is very unusual, certainly do not leave a tip. Write to the restaurant stating your dissatisfaction clearly as soon as possible.

Avoiding interruptions during the meal

▸ If you are eating at a popular restaurant frequented by colleagues, a brief wave and smile in greeting are courteous. If colleagues stop at your table, don't get weighed down in a lengthy conversation, leaving your guest to eat or drink. Introduce your guest immediately and bring the briefest of conversations to a polite close with either, 'Enjoy your meal – I'll catch up with you later' or, 'Excuse us – I'll call you.'

Talking business

▸ When discussing business during a meal, you should not produce copious amounts of paper and spread them over the dining table. Be wary also of assuming that you can begin talking business as soon as you sit down at a table. Many business people prefer to talk generally about the current economic climate or how the industry is progressing, thereby building the relationship. It is very often not until after the main course, and in some cases until the coffee stage, that specific business will be discussed.

Paying for the meal

▸ As the host, you are the person who pays. Always check before the meal that your credit cards are able to cope with the amount you will need to pay and that they are current. A friend of mine recently presented her credit card to pay a bill, only to be shouted at across the restaurant by the waiter, 'Your card has been rejected!' No discretion there. She did have another card and the presence of mind to walk up to the manager and quietly complain about the manner in which her card rejection had been handled. Most of us will have suffered the indignity of card rejection at one time or another. There is no better tip that I can give here than that you should check the limit and date status before offering a card for payment.

Here is an easy reference to guide you through the hosting a meal maze.

CHECKLIST FOR HOSTS

Do	Don't
Confirm your invitation in writing, giving details of venue, including a telephone number and directions, particularly if your guest is a new acquaintance.	Just assume your guest will be there. If you don't check, you leave yourself open to being stood up.
Ask your guest if they have any food or dietary preferences.	Believe everyone enjoys the same type of food as you do.
Book a restaurant that can accommodate your guest's tastes.	Try a new restaurant without first 'sussing out' your guest's preferences.
Arrive in time to greet your guest.	Be late.
Check how long your guest has to enjoy the meal.	Wait until halfway through the main course before checking on your guest's time availability – it's a bit late then!
Offer to book a taxi for your guest to ensure they get to their appointment on time. (Only do this if you are prepared to pay or know they are.)	Leave ordering a taxi until it's time for you to leave the restaurant.

Do	Don't
Put your guest at ease if they arrive late.	Make people feel even more embarrassed by fussing over them.
Be discreet in the way you show disappointment if a guest forgets your appointment.	Just ignore the fact that they didn't turn up.
Ask your guest where they would prefer to sit.	Sit down before your guest.
Ensure that your guest is comfortable and that they order their meal before you order yours.	Take guests to a 'new experience' and expect them to know what to order.
Attract the attention of the waiter or waitress in a quiet manner.	Click your fingers and shout … you'll wait a long time.
Complain (if necessary, and hopefully it won't be) on behalf of your guest in a discreet and courteous manner.	Announce to the entire restaurant that something is wrong.
Introduce your guest to acquaintances you may see in restaurants.	Get involved in long and complex discussions with them while your guest sits waiting for you to finish.
Be aware of when the time is right to discuss business.	Begin talking business from the moment you meet, unless that has previously been agreed with your guest.
Check you have enough money or credit to pay the bill.	Go to a restaurant that you know is out of your price range.

Being the Perfect Guest

Knowing how to behave as a guest is as important as being a good host at a business meal. If you are unsure of how to build your credibility on that front, I'll now talk you through the attributes of the perfect guest at a business meal.

When you are invited to join business colleagues or clients at a business meal, you need to know why you've been invited. Because you're good company? Yes, great, but you will usually find that a business discussion of some type will ensue, so you do need to be prepared for that. As a great boss of mine drummed into us, 'There is no such thing as a free business meal.' It doesn't make it any the less enjoyable, but it is worth remembering.

You also need to set your expectation for achieving a business result from attending. That sounds very task-oriented, but attending a business social function of any kind should be. With the combination of good personal skills and setting yourself mini-objectives, you really do build your confidence and business social reputation to a level that is noted and remembered by bosses, colleagues and clients.

Here are some tips on how to behave as a guest when dining out:

Before the meal

▸ When your host rings to check that you're still OK for tomorrow, don't snap or sound indignant – nobody is accusing you of forgetting in advance. It is a pleasantry that gives both you and your host a chance to finalise arrangements and agree how much you are looking forward to the meal.

▸ If your host hasn't asked you for your eating preferences and you are a vegetarian or have to 'stick to' a special diet, do make sure you mention it.

▶ When being entertained by a host you don't know well, make life easier for them. When they invite and you accept, include in the conversation comments about new restaurants you've heard about – it gives a host clues as to your preferences.

Dealing with preliminaries

▶ Always make sure you arrive on time. If you have agreed to meet at a restaurant, when you arrive tell the *maître d'hôtel* who greets you your name, say you are meeting your host (name), and enquire if they have arrived yet. You will then be shown to the table if your host is already there, or be asked to sit either in a separate bar area or at the table if your host hasn't arrived.

▶ Greet your host warmly, but do not become a 'hot topic'. A handshake and a comment along the lines of, 'Good to see you,' and a warm smile create the right impression.

▶ If you are delayed, make every attempt to contact your host. If your mobile phone battery is flat and there isn't a call box in sight, relax and get to the venue as soon as you can. When you arrive, apologise *once*, give a brief explanation as to why you were delayed and say that you hope the delay doesn't put pressure on your host with regard to timescales. If you are late and your host has another appointment after the meal, you should be prepared to forego pudding and coffee if necessary.

▶ If your host doesn't ask you when you arrive how long you have for the meal, do let them know your timescales, particularly if you have an appointment, so that you aren't fidgeting and eyeing your watch every few minutes if you begin to feel the meal is taking longer than you had anticipated.

▶ If you need a taxi to take you to your next destination, it's as well to mention it to your host early on so that they can organise one for you. If the host doesn't make a move to organise the taxi for you, you can make arrangements yourself. Don't assume the host will pay for the taxi if they order it for you. Yes, that's happened to me: a person hailed a taxi for me, put me in it, and sent me on my way ... I had no money. Thank heavens for hole-in-the-wall cash dispensers and a patient taxi driver.

▸ As a guest you should (female or male) be offered a choice as to where you would like to sit. If you do have a preference and the host is standing where you want to sit, a calm tone and, 'I'd prefer to sit there if I may, (name)' and then, 'Thank you' should get you the seat you prefer.

▸ As a female guest, you may be treated differently from your male colleagues in as much as many men will still stand until a woman sits; some may push your chair in behind you as you are sitting down. If this occurs, it is not the time to go into an overt feminist tirade. Just smile and say 'Thank you.'

Selecting the food

▸ When you reach the ordering stage, the host will often ask you what you'd like and order for you, although it is more usual nowadays for you to order yourself. Both ordering methods are correct.

▸ As a guest you should of course choose the dishes that tempt you but do avoid selecting the most expensive dish just for the heck of it.

Complaining discreetly

▸ If you are dissatisfied with your meal, quietly explain to your host what is wrong. Your host should then complain on your behalf (they are paying after all). However, if your host hasn't read this book and doesn't, you should quietly explain to them that you are going to complain. Raise your hand and discreetly hail the waiter. If he doesn't hear you the first time, 'Excuse me waiter' said with slightly more volume will bring him to your table. Quietly and discreetly explain your dissatisfaction, and say whether or not you would like the meal replaced. The essence is discretion. Your host will be embarrassed enough; you do not want to add to that embarrassment.

Conversing during the meal

▶ As a guest you should be guided through the 'conversation stakes' by your host. If you feel uncomfortable with a pushy approach, politely say, 'Shall we enjoy our meal before we turn to the business discussion?' and add how enjoyable the food is, and then lead the conversation on to a more general topic. You are not out to put down your host, but discussing business at an inappropriate time should be addressed. It is very usual for conversation over a business meal to cover almost every topic but business until you reach the coffee stage.

Payment issues

▶ Your host invited you, therefore he or she pays.

▶ If your host suffers an embarrassing moment because of credit-card rejection, do not sit with your mouth open watching every minute detail of the embarrassing episode; excuse yourself and visit the ladies or gents while the situation is dealt with. If, when you return, you find the situation has not been dealt with discreetly, offer to pay, adding, 'We can sort it out later' and any other non-patronising comment you believe will help the situation. If you can't help, say so and suggest you leave; your host can then handle the situation in a more private manner.

After the meal

▶ Thank your host (even if the above has happened) for the meal and occasion and make reference to a next meeting, if appropriate, before leaving the restaurant. Always write a personal note to thank your host, handwritten if possible and as soon as possible. A personal note is remembered far more than yet another e-mail.

Remember that one of the main attributes of being a perfect guest is to listen and allow your host to take the lead, even if you would do things differently.

Here is a checklist that will help build or refresh the necessary skills you require to be seen as the perfect guest.

CHECKLIST FOR GUESTS

Do	Don't
Appreciate a day-before call to check that all is well and that you will be able to attend a planned business meal.	Be defensive about such a call and see it as somebody checking up on you.
Make sure you let your host know about any special dietary or eating preferences.	Be disagreeable about a choice of restaurant if you haven't stated your likes and dislikes to your host.
Be aware of new restaurants and mention or suggest them if asked by your host.	Insist you are taken to the best or most expensive restaurant.
Be on time.	Be late through your own doing.
Let your host know your time limitations, if you have any, when you arrive at the restaurant.	Assume your host's limitations are the same as yours – you may have four hours but your host may only have two (or less), so make sure you don't outstay your welcome.

Do	Don't
Mention if you will need a taxi early in the conversation.	Expect the host to pay for the taxi.
Choose your meal with care.	Choose the most expensive item because it is just that.
Complain, if you are dissatisfied with your meal.	Shout and cause a scene.
Have a number of topics you can talk about that aren't associated with business.	Expect to discuss business until after the main course.
Be discreet if your host suffers an embarrassing moment with a credit-card rejection – yes, it's off to the ladies or gents again!	Add to the embarrassment by watching while the waiter/manager sorts it out.
Help – practically if you can – but avoid patronising behaviour if for any reason your host cannot pay the bill.	Wait around if the credit-rejection situation is proving difficult and you can't help – suggest you leave in a discreet manner.
Thank your host for the meal and occasion in person before you leave the restaurant and by writing a personal note later.	Forget to thank your host and the waiter who looked after you.

▶ Hosting and Guesting Other Events

Business entertaining can be a small or large event. The larger the event, the more preparation is needed by the host and guest, and most of you will be both host and guest at some stage during your working life. I am now going to cover the areas that need to be considered from a business etiquette (BE) perspective if an event of any kind is to be successful.

Apart from the ever-popular business meal, business enter-taining extends to receptions, buffets and attendance at cultural and sporting events. This type of business entertaining, where the social side is very evident, gives great opportunities for net-working and building business relationships; it's a business meeting of a very different kind.

Two of the main skills needed to network well are initiating conversation and circulating. These are skills that I know many people at all levels – from new-to-business to very senior – find difficult. Later in the chapter I'll cover those topics, along with dressing appropriately for the occasion, timing, arrivals and departures, and other skills that you need for more formal func-tions. But first, here are some tips on issuing invitations and replying to them.

Wording Invitations

Invitations should be as comprehensive as possible so that guests don't have to phone and enquire about dress, duration and so on. The following minimum information should be included:

▶ From whom

▶ To whom

▶ Type of occasion

▶ Date

▶ Times

▶ Venue

▶ Dress

▶ RSVP and address

If you do not specify the dress code on your invitation, it is assumed that women will wear a short dress, evening trousers or a skirt suit, and men will wear a suit (*see* also dress code, *page 192*).

For example:

Sir Bryce Fowler, KBE, Chairman of Fowler International Ltd, has pleasure in inviting

Mr and Mrs Peter Guest

to a reception to celebrate the publication of *The Fowler Story* at Fleming House, 33 Etiquette Road, Brighton BN1 2BE 4.00 to 6.00 p.m. on Tuesday, 5 July 2003

RSVP Ms Elizabeth Bush, at Fleming House and on 0001 8888

Wording Reply Cards

Where necessary, a reply card can be enclosed together with a stamped, addressed envelope containing at least the following details:

Mr and Mrs Peter Guest of PG Ltd

are able/unable to attend your reception to celebrate the publication of *The Fowler Story* on 5 July 2003

Replying to Invitations

Replies to invitations should be as prompt as possible. An **acceptance** can take the following form:

Dear Ms Bush,

Thank you for the invitation from Sir Bryce Fowler to attend the reception to celebrate the publication of *The Fowler Story*. My wife, Lorna, and I are very happy to accept.

Yours sincerely,

Peter Guest

Refusals should contain the reason why:

Dear Ms Bush,

Thank you very much for the invitation from Sir Bryce Fowler to attend the reception celebrating the publication of *The Fowler Story*. Unfortunately, I will be out of town on that day, and so, with regret am unable to attend. My wife and I hope the occasion and the book will both be a great success.

Yours sincerely,

Peter Guest

A formal **third person** reply may be used to invitations from people you don't have a personal acquaintance with:

Dear Ms Bush,

Mr Peter Guest is [e.g.] abroad on business and has asked me to thank you for your invitation to the reception celebrating the publication of *The Fowler Story*. [Either:] He is pleased to accept and looks forward to meeting Sir Bryce and Lady Fowler on 5 July. [Or:] He very much regrets that due to a prior arrangement he is unable to change, he will not be able to attend.

Yours sincerely,

Horace Henry
Personal Assistant to Mr Peter Guest

Dressing for the Occasion

Once you have accepted an invitation, dressing for the occasion needs to be considered – yes, men as well. Most invitations will state on them the dress code for the event. If an invitation states 'black tie' it doesn't mean *only* that. I think it's worth mentioning here that if you are in any doubt at all as to the expected dress for the occasion, you should ring the organisers. I nearly always do – I learnt the hard way. An escort assured me that a long, full and flowing dress was absolutely right for a reception we had to attend – wrong. Just ask me who was the *only* person in long.

The following is a general guideline for most business social gatherings, from the informal to the extremely formal.

Type of event	Women	Men
Evening cocktail reception or dinner.	Short black dress (never, ever lets you down). Evening trousers or skirt suit.	Dark suit, plain shirt and a tie of your choice. Black shoes and dark socks.
Black tie – formal.	Short or full-length evening dress.	Evening dress suit. Braces not belts are worn with dinner jackets. Black shoes (some men choose patent).
White tie – very formal.	Ball gown. Long gloves.	Tails, stiff shirt, wing collar and stud, waistcoat, piqué tie, black patent shoes and white gloves.

There are other dress codes but these will see you through most formal occasions (I have covered specifics in Chapter 17).

Timing Your Arrival and Departure

Your invitation will state what time you need to arrive at an event. If the word 'sharp' appears after the time – for example '6.30 p.m. sharp' – that is exactly what it means.

The timing that can cause confusion is, for example, '7.30 p.m. for 8.00 p.m.' Don't think you can arrive five minutes before 8.00 p.m. The whole idea is to give you, as a guest, time to mingle before being called for dinner, and you normally do this 15 minutes before 8.00 p.m. This ensures that you are ready for the formalities/dinner to begin on time at 8.00 p.m. If your invitation states that the reception you are attending starts at

8.00 p.m., the accepted time of arrival for guests is ten minutes after the stated time. And when the 'party' is over – leave. The time of a reception is usually clearly marked on an invitation. If you only have a start time, watch for clues that signal the end: drying up of drink, hosts standing by the door – you know the type of thing.

As You Arrive

When you arrive at formal functions, you will often be announced by the Master of Ceremonies (MC). He will ask you your name, and announce you as you arrive at a greeting line, where your hosts will welcome you. The greeting line is not the place to linger and chat – a brief, 'Good evening,' or if you know people well, 'How good to see you again' as you shake hands and move on is all that's needed.

Making Conversation

Now comes the bit a lot of you dread – initiating conversation, small talk and circulating. Many people dislike the thought of making small talk because they believe the only topics you talk about are the weather and your journey – well, if all else fails, they are useful!

▶ Have a number of topics you feel you can confidently begin a conversation with:

The surroundings	Films
Sport	Favourite people and places
Music	News items
World affairs	Business associations
Holidays	Industry 'happenings'
Food	

▶ Always read a daily newspaper to ensure that you are up to date with business news and current affairs.

▶ Avoid *initiating* a conversation on politics and religion, and asking questions of a personal nature, for example regarding income, sex and family.

▶ If you tend to speak quickly, remember to pause now and again – make it easy for people to listen to you.

▶ When discussing business, avoid gossip. Be loyal to the company, department and your colleagues, and be sensitive to the reactions of others.

▶ Remember that conversation is two-way and good listeners are often known as some of the best conversationalists. When conversing, show real interest in the person you are talking to. The minute your mind wanders, you will show the person you are talking to that you have lost interest, and they will notice. Do not interrupt others or overtalk them when they are speaking, or finish their sentences for them. Encourage the person you are talking to with such phrases as:

   ▶ 'That's interesting; where did you see that?'
   ▶ 'I noticed an article about your company in …'
   ▶ 'So tell me when you decided to …'
   ▶ 'When do you think that will happen to …?'

▶ Give some thought to developing some links of your own. Empathising with others soon builds a relationship. You can say:

   ▶ 'I appreciate that feeling.'
   ▶ 'Yes, it's difficult isn't it? How will …?'
   ▶ 'That must be really exciting …'
   ▶ 'When will you be able to …?'

It makes the person you are talking to feel comfortable because you are building empathy, not just talking about subjects that are of particular interest to you.

Circulating

When you attend a business reception or business social event of any kind, it is worth remembering that the event is for cultivating contacts and developing relationships. Circulating enables you to meet, cultivate and maintain as many business relationships as possible. When you walk into a room full of people who are already conversing in clusters and you don't know any of them, there is no easy way. You have to walk up to a group, introduce yourself and start a conversation. The more you do it, the easier it becomes.

▸ If you feel confident and project confidence through your body language and tone of voice, other people will feel relaxed in your company and want to know more about you. However, if you feel awkward and show that you are nervous, people will perceive you to be unsure of yourself and will feel ill at ease speaking to you – it's a vicious circle.

▸ Continuously move from one person to another. You will speak with some people for 20 minutes or more. With others, you'll move on after five minutes.

▸ Pay attention to body language. When you walk into a room, if you strut you are exhibiting arrogance; if you walk with your head down you look very unsure of yourself. People can be put off because you are not projecting a relaxed confidence in either case.

▸ When you stand and talk to people, it is important to be relaxed and natural, with your weight evenly distributed. Don't fidget from one foot to the other.

▸ If you stand with your arms crossed, you are really giving people a 'no communication wanted here' message. You may want to use this technique if you are trapped by a bore or if someone is encroaching on your space and you feel uncomfortable, but not if you want to be accepted and to encourage someone to speak.

▸ Ask your host for information about the interests of the other guests. It's always useful to have an idea of who will be attending a function and it enables you to initiate conversation more easily.

▸ Try to lead a shy person into conversation. If you notice someone hanging back, ask their opinion about a topic.

▸ Let any newcomer joining your cluster into the secret of what you have been talking about; for example, 'Oh, hallo Jane, we are just discussing who we think will win the Gold Cup at Cheltenham next month – who do you think will do it?'

▸ When circulating, the manner in which you disengage yourself from a conversation is important. You shouldn't finish a sentence and move away from someone without making a comment such as:

> ▸ 'Excuse me, I have just seen someone I must catch up with …'
> ▸ 'It's been good seeing you again. Oh, there's [name] – I need to speak to her. Excuse me …'
> ▸ 'We must circulate. Do you know [name]? Oh, let me introduce you …'
> ▸ 'I've enjoyed meeting you. Excuse me I must speak to [name].'

The important thing is – say something before you move on, as long as it is polite.

▸Impromptu Speaking

There is one other topic I'd like to cover before I give you a checklist for business entertaining, and that is how to deliver a vote of thanks. You may never need to do this, but just in case somebody asks you out of the blue – it does happen – to say thank you on behalf of the guests at a reception or informal event, here are a few tips for you.

Don't believe you have to talk for ten minutes at least – you don't. Being sincere, clear and concise are the three key points to delivering a good vote of thanks. Be sure you know who's at the event. If dignitaries are there you need to address them correctly (see Chapter 18).

I spoke earlier of using the past, present and future technique (*see page 48*) – it comes in really handy at times like these. A vote-of-thanks example:

(Dignitaries) 'Ladies and Gentlemen. It gives me great pleasure to propose the vote of thanks on behalf of the guests. When I was invited ...

Past   '... to this event, I, like most of you I am sure, was intrigued by the choice of venue – a castle which is steeped in history and such an important ...

Present   ' ... tourist attraction for our business community. The reception this evening has been wonderful. The food and local wines have been delicious, and we've all had the opportunity to get to know one another in a relaxed and hospitable atmosphere. Our warmest thanks, Mr Kelly, ...

Future   ' ... to you and your company, ABC Travel, for a really enjoyable evening. We all look forward to working with you and ABC next year.'

I hope this formula works for you. It has certainly worked for many others – it can be used to get your thoughts together quickly if you are the person suddenly asked to:

▸ Welcome guests on behalf of your company.

▸ Introduce a distinguished speaker.

▶ Present an award.

to name but three instances.

And now the dos and don'ts of business entertaining.

CHECKLIST FOR BUSINESS ENTERTAINING

Do	Don't
Use events to network and cultivate business relationships.	Attend events just to eat and drink large amounts.
Ensure guests know what they are expected to wear when you invite them to an event.	Leave sending the invitation until a month before an event. In business, invitations should be sent a minimum of six weeks, if possible three months, prior to the event.
Reply promptly to an invitation, whether it's with a 'yes' or a 'no' – the organiser will appreciate knowing as soon as possible.	Just telephone to accept or decline – always send a written reply.
Adhere to an invitation's timing instructions when 'sharp' appears on it.	Be late.
Leave at a reasonable time, when it is clear the event is over.	Be a hanger-on and outstay your welcome – go!
Speak clearly when giving your name to an MC for a greeting line.	Linger and chat as you move along a greeting line – you'll cause a people jam.
Have a number of topics with which you can initiate conversation.	Initiate conversation on topics such as religion and politics, or ask personal questions.

Do	Don't
Read a daily newspaper to keep you updated on current affairs and business news.	Let your mind wander when talking to others – it gives the impression that you've lost interest.
Encourage others to speak.	Overtalk or interrupt others.
Talk with people rather than at them.	Gossip about your company or colleagues.
Circulate and meet as many people as possible.	Stay in company clusters.
Be sincere, clear and concise when delivering a vote of thanks or welcoming speech.	Go off at a tangent or demean yourself and others.
Have a strong beginning and ending.	Babble on and on and on.
Take business cards with you.	Leave your mobile phone switched on.

Preparation is key if an event is to be successful and if you are to get the most from these networking opportunities. Knowing something about the people who will be attending, and about the event itself, will make initiating conversation and circulating easier. Being well versed in your own company's achievements will also make you feel more confident. And while you are busy circulating and meeting new people, if you say you will contact a person after the event, do so!

I've covered general business entertaining, so in the next chapter I will deal with specific events, invitations to which are recognised as being a real bonus. This chapter and Chapter 18 cover events and conventions that are specific to the UK, so move to Chapter 19 if they are not currently relevant to you.

CHAPTER 17

Attending Prestigious Events

No longer is entry to royal events, first nights and major sporting events exclusive to a few of the privileged and celebrities. Corporate sponsorship has opened the doors to many exciting and glamorous business entertaining opportunities. I won't cover every event here, but will give you an insight into what to do and, in some cases, what not to do, when attending recognised prestigious events.

I am going to begin with the only event in the social calendar that cannot be bought into by corporate sponsorship – the Royal garden party.

▶ Royal Garden Party

This is one of the most prestigious events you could be invited to attend.

The Invitation

The Lord Chamberlain sends the invitation on behalf of the monarch. You do not have to reply to confirm your acceptance. The enclosed admission card should be used if the invitation is being declined. Royal invitations are in the nature of commands, so if you cannot attend, you should have a very good reason or you may be erased from future guest lists.

All you need to know to find, park and wander over the imperial pastures at the rear of Buckingham Palace will be contained within the invitation.

Cameras are not allowed unless specially authorised. Umbrellas are not allowed either, so just hope and pray that it doesn't rain.

Dress Code

Women wear smart dresses, with or without jackets, or suits with skirts or trousers. Trousers and shirts are acceptable, as is national costume or uniform – and hats.

Men dress formally: morning suits (reserve yours well in advance if you are hiring and want it to fit), lounge suits or uniform, but preferably no mayoral chains of office.

Traditional Timetable

3.15 p.m. The gates open. If you arrive an hour early, the queue will already be about a quarter of a mile long, so be prepared for a long, slow shuffle.

4.00 p.m. The Royal Family appears. They walk through the gardens along an avenue of guests, stopping and chatting occasionally. If special presentations are to be held, they make their way to the appropriate area.

5.00 p.m. After general mingling, the Royal Family go off to their own tent for tea. Guests are shown into other tea tents around the garden.

6.00 p.m. The drums will roll, spines will stiffen and the

National Anthem will be played. The Royals will depart, leaving you to start your shuffle towards the exit. It is permissible to leave early by arranging your departure through a member of staff.

Personal Presentation

You will not suddenly be plucked from the crowd to be presented; you will have been forewarned. A member of the Royal household will have made contact in advance and gleaned a few details about yourself, such as whether you have achieved particular prominence in your field and whether you have met any of the Royals before. As the due time approaches, you will be told where to be, when to be there and what to do when you arrive and when you are to be presented to the Queen.

Royal garden parties are tightly organised, and leave virtually nothing to chance. The guest's only responsibility is to speak when spoken to by a Royal.

Nerves should not be too great an issue when 'that' moment arrives. The Royal Family are accustomed to making allowances for the sudden change in condition of a guest when engaged in a Royal tête-à-tête. Relax and enjoy your special moment.

What to say

▶ The Queen is addressed as 'Your majesty,' and subsequently as 'Ma'am' (pronounced 'Mam'); the Duke of Edinburgh as 'Your Royal Highness,' and subsequently as 'Sir.'

▶ All other members of the Royal Family are addressed initially as 'Your Royal Highness' and subsequently as 'Sir' or 'Ma'am.'

▶ A king would be addressed as 'Your majesty' and subsequently as 'Sir,' and his queen as 'Your majesty' and 'Ma'am.'

▶ Men should bow and women curtsey when being introduced and when taking leave of royalty.

▶ If royalty do engage you in conversation, it will probably be about your job or the party itself. So it's worth rehearsing a short statement.

When presented to royalty, the simple rule is not to speak first. That is their prerogative. Don't be disappointed if they break off quickly, as their movements are usually timed to the second.

What to do

A royal hand, if proffered, should be lightly and briefly taken. At the same time, men should bow from the neck only; women either curtsey (not a full-bodied collapse) or bow their head.

▶ Royal Ascot

Since it was established in 1711 by Queen Anne, Royal Ascot has been a leading event of the London season. It is the only race-course in the country still owned by the Crown, and the only sporting event which the Queen herself and members of her family attend on a daily basis. Their carriage procession through the Golden Gate and along the straight mile signals the start of each day's racing.

Much business entertaining goes on, often organised by corporate hospitality firms who provide champagne receptions, morning coffee and afternoon tea, luncheons with all the trimmings, car-park passes and entry tickets to the Grandstands.

Tickets are issued by the Ascot Office at St James's Palace. Applications begin in January. Further information on ticket procedures is published the previous month in the court pages of *The Times* and *Daily Telegraph*.

The Royal Enclosure

Strict rules are applied from the start. When first applying for a Royal Enclosure badge, you will be sent a sponsor form, which must be signed by someone who is known personally to the Queen or who has received vouchers to attend Royal Ascot at least four times before. Even if you can fulfil these conditions, your application will not guarantee tickets. Admission is entirely at the discretion of Her Majesty's representative. He may bar people of bad reputation, bankrupts, those with criminal records and so on.

Dress in the Royal Enclosure is formal. Those improperly dressed will simply not be admitted. Men should wear morning suits and top hats, women wear smart day dresses. Hats are a must for women.

Cameras are prohibited. Members of the Royal Family must not be pointed at, stared at or approached, particularly not for racing tips!

Behaviour is expected to be discreet. Being in the Royal Enclosure at Ascot means not screaming loudly when your horse is winning and certainly not when it's losing.

Switch off your mobile phone.

▶ Horse Racing (General)

The Jockey Club is the governing body of flat racing, and the season runs from the end of March to the middle of November. National Hunt, or steeplechasing, is governed by the National Hunt Committee, and runs from August to the following Whitsun; it includes the Grand National at Aintree. Other important courses are at Epsom, Newmarket, Goodwood, Doncaster, Sandown Park, York and Ascot.

The three enclosures are: the Club or Members', Tattersall's and the Silver Ring. Men should wear suits, and women smart clothes. In winter, make sure they are warm. Hats are optional.

Many businesses hire marquees for their guests and provide a champagne buffet or picnic. Watching the horses is optional. Some companies sponsor races and prizes, or run concurrent charity drives. Supporting such events as generously as possible is fun; otherwise, it is inadvisable to be seen placing large bets by clients or employees.

▶ Henley Regatta

Established over a century and a half ago, and held at the height of summer, Henley Regatta is one of the most colourful sporting events of the year. It is necessary to arrive very early to avoid massive traffic jams. It is a good idea to book into one of the town's lovely old hotels for the previous night to avoid hassle at the beginning of the day.

The Enclosures

Entrance to the Stewards' Enclosure is by invitation only. You pay at the gate to get in to the Regatta Enclosure.

Dress in the enclosures may seem casual, but it is strictly regulated. Men wear lounge suits, blazers or jackets, with grey, beige or white trousers, and ties or cravats. Women wear dresses or suits with a hemline *below* the knee. Women will not be admitted wearing divided skirts or trousers of any kind, or skirts and blouses. No one is admitted wearing shorts with T-shirts or any form of casual top, and certainly not jeans.

Behaviour is English: restrained. One does not shout. Not a lot of cheering goes on. Refined applause is more the mark. Getting legless and starting to sing rugger songs is a cue for a selection of the 40 elected Henley stewards to eject the offender before the second verse.

Costly buffet lunches and drinks are served in a marquee, and people try not to get caught drinking anything other than 'champers' or Pimms. Picnicking outside the enclosure is permitted and has become something of a tradition.

It is advisable to leave late. Consider dining at one of the restaurants in the area before motoring back through thinning traffic.

No mobile phones are allowed.

▶Cowes

Located on the northern tip of the Isle of Wight, Cowes can be reached easily on foot, or by car, train or coach via passenger ferry – or by yacht, of course. Once there, lunching, dining and posing on the deck of a sponsored or chartered yacht is the way many corporate entertainers and entertainees enjoy this classic regatta week.

Ten thousand or so yachtsmen sail up and down the Solent during Cowes week, which usually starts at the beginning of August.

You can regard the Cowes schedule in one of two ways: either the sport starts at 9.30 a.m. and is followed by socialising at nightly yacht club balls and champagne binges, or everything starts in the evenings and ends in the early hours in time for the participants to change out of their dinner jackets or party dresses and into their pumps and lifejackets and fall into their yachts. Either way, it's a stimulating and exhausting experience, but with a rigid and restricted social structure.

Everything centres on a handful of yacht clubs. Entry to the clubs' premises and to parties on their members' vessels is by invitation only. Temporary membership of most of them will smooth the social passage. This may be obtained by applying to the yacht clubs' secretaries. The Royal Yacht Squadron (RYS) membership, however, is obtainable only through the introduction of an existing member. The RYS is extremely formal: women wear dresses and, occasionally, hats, and most of the men sport a collar and black or navy tie with a yachting suit or reefer jacket, and white or grey trousers. (Invitations will state what form of dress is required.) The same dress is worn in other clubs, although women do not often wear hats and can wear smart trousers.

▶ Lord's Cricket Ground

Lord's cricket ground is the home of the Marylebone Cricket Club (MCC) and of the regulatory body of English cricket.

The Pavilion

Unless otherwise advised, men must wear jacket, collar and tie when attending the Pavilion at Lord's.

Cameras should not be in evidence.

For men who enjoy one another's company, the Pavilion is a relaxing place to spend the day. A smattering of clapping, a hum of comment and the occasional yelp of excitement are the accepted level of applause and appreciation. Shouting is seriously frowned upon and could get the offender thrown out.

Prolonged booing or jeering is always bad form and very bad manners at any sporting event.

Public Areas

Spectators in the public areas are quite self-controlled too, except when England plays the West Indies, at which time there is a constant happy sound. The Ashes matches against Australia are renowned for the wit and language of the expatriates in the crowd.

Tickets

This is the world's greatest cricket club, and demand for tickets, especially for test matches, is always high. Members apply for them in January; they become available to the public in March.

▶ Wimbledon

The All England Club at Wimbledon circulates booking details of its summer open tournament in December the previous year. Obtaining tickets can be pot luck, unless you are an All England Club member or belong to a club recognised by the Lawn Tennis Association (LTA), or your company is a business sponsor.

The members' enclosure is an elegant location where jackets and ties and generally smart dress are obligatory, and where conversation is muted so as not to distract the players. The most prestigious Wimbledon tickets are for the centre court on the men's or women's final day, but the men's and women's semi-finals day is sometimes the more exhilarating.

If you and your guests intend eating at Wimbledon and indulging in the traditional strawberries and cream, make sure your waistline and budget can handle them.

▶ Playing Golf

Contrary to popular legend and executive pleading, a golf course is not the best setting in which to hack out business deals. It is a place better suited to building relationships and for creative thinking. Three hours or so playing golf in pleasant surroundings is conducive to formulating new ideas. Deals, if they are to be concluded, are best left until after the eighteenth hole. Company handicap tournaments, too, are excellent opportunities for executives to establish closer relationships with colleagues and clients.

As with purely recreational golf, if you are an inept or inexperienced player you should not suggest a game with a mustard-keen, low handicap client. Thrashing a ball in assorted directions and disappearing for long periods to retrieve it is an imposition on your client's patience and goodwill. If your golf isn't up to scratch, you'd be much wiser taking your client to one of the large golfing tournaments.

▶ Opera and Ballet

These are occasions for truly elegant and certainly expensive business entertaining. The cream of English opera is performed at the Royal Opera House, as is some of the best ballet. You need to book months ahead for the most prestigious performances and artists. To enjoy them in real style, a box should be reserved. Booking seats elsewhere may submit your business guests to the scrum that takes place in the crush bars during the intervals. It is much more agreeable to close the door of the box and enjoy a plate of smoked salmon sandwiches and a bottle of champagne served by your own waiter.

A really important point to remember if you are sitting in a box and enjoying wine or champagne with your buffet supper is to *never* put a glass on the ledge of the box; it is a very definite no-no.

At ballet and opera gala nights at the Royal Opera House, as well as at other theatres, black tie and evening dresses are worn. At other times, suits and smart dresses are appropriate.

Latecoming is dealt with ruthlessly after curtain-up: the latecomers are made to wait until a suitable pause in the performance, which could be at the end of the first act.

Arriving early is certainly a good idea, as it enables you to book refreshments for the interval. More importantly, it gives you time to read the programme notes so you know what is happening on stage.

Timing your applause can be tricky. Dedicated opera and ballet lovers restrain themselves from clapping before the dying notes of a piece. But how do you know when the end is nigh? You don't, unless you have seen it before. So newcomers should follow the lead of others.

▶ Concerts

You need not dress formally, just smartly, for most classical concerts. Arriving late is not on; you will certainly be barred from entrance until the end of a piece.

Noise is totally unacceptable to classical concert audiences. Rustling paper, whispering or – heaven forbid – humming along will engender hostility from all around; you'll get no sympathy if you cough or wheeze either.

If you are a newcomer to concerts and unsure whether to applaud or not – and it can be confusing – wait until the majority of the audience applauds.

It is advisable to reserve drinks for the interval if you don't want to face long queues and short tempers. Book taxis for the end of the performance to avoid similar problems.

▶ Theatre

Not only does London's West End brim with theatres, but also there are many outstanding outer London and provincial companies all offering excellent opportunities for business entertaining and sponsorship.

The best seats are in the front ten rows of the stalls or in the front five of the dress circle. Boxes may be prestigious, but in many theatres they do not give a full view of the stage – short of grasping your valued client by the ankles as they lean out for a better look.

Organise interval drinks before the show starts and, if possible, reserve a table in the bar. Many shows end at about 10.00 p.m., so it is a reasonable idea to suggest – and then book – supper to follow.

▶ Exhibition Openings

Sharing an invitation with a client to the opening of an art exhibition is a smart move. They can be cosy and prestigious affairs, often incorporating an exclusive invited guest list.

You should arrive on time, as many contemporary exhibition openings begin with a speech by the artist. The catalogue will contain background information on the artist, which is worth reading in case you are introduced and wish to say something meaningful.

The atmosphere will vary according to the gallery, but you should be prepared for behaviour ranging from the intense and cryptic to the colourful and bizarre.

▶ Charity Galas

These occasions can take the form of a concert, a ball, a cabaret or a dinner. They are the most prestigious, glittering and expensive occasions of the social calendar and may be attended by the royal and the renowned.

There is a London gala circuit attended by the same people night after night, so such occasions can be elitist and cliquey. If you are unconnected, it is best to go with your own clique of at least four people.

You should wear the smartest of evening wear and accessories and should be lavish in your generosity to the cause. Many people tend to behave in a flashy manner when contributing money on these occasions. Those who give from the heart are the quietest about it.

▶ The Queen's Awards for Enterprise

This is an accolade which you do not wait to be invited to or sponsored for. You apply yourself. The Queen's Award is by far the UK's most prestigious business honour. It is meticulously administered and monitored. Representatives of the winners attend a Buckingham Palace reception, and a dignitary visits the winners' premises for an on-site presentation ceremony.

The awards are made annually on the Queen's personal birthday – 12 April. They are valid for five years. There are currently three categories: international trade, innovation and sustainable development.

The Queen grants the awards on the advice of the Prime Minister and an advisory committee made up of representatives from industry, commerce, the trade unions and government departments.

The company can display the award emblem on company goods, packaging, livery and stationery. It can also fly the award's flag for five years.

The winning criteria are:

For export: in the international trade category 'substantial and sustained increase in overseas earnings and in commercial success to a level which is outstanding for the goods or services concerned and for the size of the applicant's operations'.

For innovation: 'innovation resulting in substantial improvement in business performance and commercial success to a level which is outstanding for the goods or services concerned and for the size of the applicant's operations'.

For sustainable development: 'sustainable development contributing to substantial improvement in business performance and commercial success to a level which is outstanding for the goods or services concerned and for the size of the applicant's operations'.

Application forms and guidance notes are obtainable from the Queen's Awards mailing house, telephone number 08705 134486. Remember to say which of the three categories you need application forms for.

If you are granted the Queen's Award, your organisation will be invited to Buckingham Palace for a reception given by the Queen.

At a mutually convenient time, the Queen's representative, the Lord Lieutenant, will visit the company or organisation for the presentation ceremony. It is customary for a lunch or buffet to be organised, and as many of the workforce as possible, particularly all of those who have contributed to achieving the honour, should attend the ceremony.

It isn't only when you are presented to royalty that you need to have an awareness of how to address people correctly. Many of you will find yourselves in situations where you need to address titled people in person or in writing. The following chapter will act as a reference for the times when you are unsure of how to address dignitaries.

CHAPTER **18**

Addressing Dignitaries

I f you are representing your company, you may well meet titled
people and other dignitaries, and it is as well to know how to
address them. I dealt with addressing royalty on page 203 and
here's how to address a whole host of other people who have an
official rank or status.

▶ Dukes and Below

Order of seniority:

Royal duke (direct relative of the Queen)

Duke

Marquess

Earl

Viscount

Baron

Baronet

Knight

At formal affairs, royal dukes and duchesses are presented with their full titles: 'His Royal Highness the Duke of Somewhere.' They are addressed as 'Your Royal Highness' initially, and thereafter as 'Your Grace' or 'Sir/Ma'am.'

Lesser dukes are presented as 'The Duke of Somewhere' and are addressed as 'Your Grace' or 'Duke.' Their wives are addressed as 'Duchess,' then 'Your Grace' or 'Ma'am.'

Dowager duchesses (widows) are presented as 'Duchess Surname.' In writing they should be called 'The Dowager Duchess of Somewhere.' They should be addressed as 'Duchess.'

The sons and daughters of dukes are lords and ladies. Depending on their age, their title is used with their first name, that is 'Lord/Lady Firstname.'

Marquesses (or marquis) and marchionesses, viscounts and viscountesses, barons and baronesses, and earls and countesses are addressed by their titles or as 'Your Lordship/Ladyship' and 'Lord/Lady Surname.'

The sons of marquesses are 'Your Lordship' or 'Lord Surname.' The children of earls are 'The Hon. Firstname Surname' but are addressed without titles.

A baronet and a knight are 'Sir Firstname'; their wives are 'Lady Surname.'

A dame – the female equivalent of a knight – is normally addressed as 'Dame Firstname'; her husband has no corresponding title.

Politicians

The Prime Minister is addressed by title.

Government ministers are addressed as 'Minister.'

MPs are addressed by name.

The Clergy

The Pope is addressed as 'Your Holiness.'

Cardinals are addressed by title (i.e. 'Cardinal') or as 'Your Eminence.'

Archbishops are addressed by title or as 'Your Grace.'

Anglican and Roman Catholic bishops are addressed by title or as 'My Lord.'

Most other clergy are addressed by their titles; for example, Rabbi, Canon, Monsignor, Vicar, Father Somebody, etc.

▶ Courtesy Titles

Mayoralty

London, Belfast, Cardiff, Dublin and York all have lord mayors. They are presented as 'The Rt. Hon. Lord Mayor of Somewhere.' They and all other lord mayors are addressed as '(My) Lord Mayor.'

A mayor is addressed as 'Your Worship,' 'Mayor Somebody' or 'Mr Mayor.' His wife (or daughter if she fulfils the official function) is presented as 'Lady Mayoress.'

Lady Mayors are also known as mayoresses and addressed as 'Your Worship,' 'Mayor Somebody' or 'Madam Mayor.'

Aberdeen, Dundee, Edinburgh and Glasgow each have a lord provost. They are addressed as 'Provost,' 'My Lord,' 'Your Lordship' or 'Mr Chairman,' or the female equivalents.

Aldermen and councillors are addressed as 'Alderman Surname' and 'Councillor Surname.'

Further Reference
The most comprehensive source of titles and forms of address
can be found in *Debrett's Correct Form*, edited by Patrick
Montague-Smith and published by Headline.

▶ Upwardly Mobile Letters

Letters to senior establishment figures should be addressed as
follows. They all, except for the Pope, should be signed off
'Yours sincerely'. (Names or places have been added to titles to
clarify usage.)

Royalty

Letters to HM The Queen/HRH The Duke of Edinburgh (when
the sender is not previously known to them), are all addressed
to the relevant Private Secretary:
The Private Secretary to Her Majesty The Queen/His Royal
Highness The Duke of Edinburgh
Begin: Dear Private Secretary

Letters to HRH The Prince of Wales/HRH The Princess Royal
are addressed to:
His Royal Highness The Prince of Wales/Her Royal Highness
The Princess Royal
Begin: Your Royal Highness

Letters to royal dukes/duchesses are addressed to:
His/Her Royal Highness, The Duke/Duchess of Kent
Begin: Your Royal Highness

Peers, Baronets, Knights

Letters to dukes/duchesses are addressed to:

The Duke/Duchess of Oxland
Begin: Dear Duke/Duchess of Oxland, or Dear Duke/Duchess

Letters to marquesses/marchionesses, earls/countesses,
viscounts/viscountesses are addressed to:
The Marquess/Marchioness of Parsham, The Earl/Countess of
Satham, The Viscount/Viscountess Tatham
Begin: Dear Lord/Lady Parsham/Satham/Tatham

Letters to barons/baronesses are addressed to:
The Lord Makepiece/The Lady Makepiece
Begin: Dear Lord/Lady Makepiece

Letters to baronets and their wives are addressed to:
Sir Anthony Dewit, Bt/Lady Dewit
Begin: Dear Sir Anthony/Lady Dewit

Letters to life peers are addressed to:
The Lord Fireback/The Lady Fireback
Begin: Dear Lord/Lady Fireback

Letters to knights and their wives are addressed to:
Sir Charles Counter/Lady Counter
Begin: Dear Sir Charles/Lady Counter

Letters to hereditary peeresses (direct line) are addressed to:
The Countess of Downe
Begin: Dear Lady Downe

Letters to life peeresses are addressed to:
Baroness Chambers
Begin: Dear Lady Chambers

Letters to dames are addressed to:
Dame Flora Lynch
Begin: Dear Dame Flora

The Clergy

Letters to (Anglican) lord archbishops are addressed to:
The Most Revd and Rt. Hon. the Lord Archbishop of
Canterbury/York
Begin: Dear Archbishop

Letters to (Anglican) bishops are addressed to:
The Rt. Revd the Lord Bishop of Birmingham
(The Bishop of London is addressed as: The Rt. Revd and
Rt. Hon. the Lord Bishop of London)
Begin: Dear Bishop

Letters to Anglican vicars are addressed to:
Reverend Michael Waters
Begin: Dear Mr Waters or Dear Father Waters

Letters to Roman Catholic priests are addressed to:
The Revd Seamus O'Connell
Begin: Dear Father O'Connell

Letters to Church of Scotland ministers are addressed to:
The Revd Dougal McMillan
Begin: Dear Mr McMillan

Letters to the Pope are addressed to:
His Holiness The Pope
Begin: Your Holiness or Most Holy Father
The letter should end: I have the honour to remain your
Holiness's most devoted and obedient child (or most humble
child). A non-Roman Catholic may replace 'child' by 'servant'.

Letters to cardinals are addressed to:
Dear Cardinal Murphy or Your Eminence

Letters to (Roman Catholic) archbishops are addressed to:
His Grace the Archbishop of Beltown
Begin: Dear Archbishop or Your Grace

Letters to The Chief Rabbi are addressed to:
The Chief Rabbi Mr Emantiel Foreman
Begin: Dear Chief Rabbi

Politicians (personal and official letters)

Letters to the Prime Minister are addressed to:
The Rt. Hon. Paddy Stitch PC, MP
Begin: Dear Prime Minister

Letters to the Chancellor of the Exchequer are addressed to:
The Rt. Hon. James Sargeant, PC, MP
Begin: Dear Chancellor

Letters to Secretaries of State are addressed to:
The Rt. Hon. Glynis Morris, PC, MP
The Home Secretary/Foreign Secretary, etc.
Begin: Dear Secretary of State/Home Secretary/Foreign
Secretary, etc.

Letters to ministers are addressed to:
Title or Peter Dough, Esq., MP
Begin: Dear Minister

Letters to backbenchers are addressed to:
Thomas Flack, Esq., MP
Begin: Dear Mr Flack

Local Government

(NB: Don't confuse a lady mayor with a lady mayoress – the
latter is the 'consort' of her husband, the mayor, while the
former is mayor in her own right.)

Letters to lord and lady mayors are addressed to:
The Rt. Hon. the Lord Mayor of
Belfast/Cardiff/Dublin/London/York, and for other cities:

The Right Worshipful the Lord Mayor of ...
Begin: Dear Lord Mayor (including Lady Mayors)

Letters to lady mayoresses are addressed to:
The Lady Mayoress of ...
Begin: Dear Lady Mayoress

Letters to mayors/mayoresses (or mayor's consort) of only the following places are addressed to:
The Worshipful the Mayor/Mayoress of Hastings/Hythe/
Liverpool/New Romney/Rye,
and letters to mayors/mayoresses (or mayor's consort) of other places are addressed to:
The Worshipful the Mayor/Lady Mayoress of (borough or equivalent)
Begin: Dear Mr Mayor/Madam Mayoress

For those of you who travel, the quick-reference guide that follows will ensure your continuous upward mobility around the globe.

CHAPTER 19

Foreign Business Etiquette

This is a quick-reference guide to the business etiquette and customs of leading business territories. Its purpose is to smooth your way through your business trips, and to help you make the most profitable first and lasting impressions with foreign business associates on their home ground.

In some countries, etiquette may vary by area; in these cases I have adhered as much as possible to advice that is generally sound for a country's most important business regions. I have tried not to fall into the trap of being over-prescriptive – bear in mind that the advice given is general and will not apply in all cases.

Wherever you go:

▶ Always prepare well beforehand.

▶ Build empathy.

▶ Listen and concentrate on what is being said.

▶ Accept business customs rather than judge them.

▶ Don't assume or imply that your way of doing things is always the best.

The following countries and regions are included in this section:

Arab World
Argentina
Australia
Belgium
China
France
Germany
India
Ireland
Italy
Japan

Korea, South
Netherlands
Poland
Russia
Singapore
Spain
Sweden
Switzerland
United Kingdom
USA

Arab World

Business tips
Appointments are generally made as an indication that a meeting will take place; punctuality is not considered a key virtue. Major business decisions are made at the highest level, but they are not necessarily made by those with whom you are negotiating, and they can take a long time. The art of negotiation is based on taking time, compromising and on no one losing face.

Formalities
Business cards should be printed in both languages. Business meetings are generally cordial, but beware of overfamiliarity. Do not discuss politics, religion or sex. Before discussing business, it is normal to exchange pleasantries and enjoy tea or coffee. Integrity is essential and it is expected that one's word will be kept to the letter.

The ninth month of the Muslim calendar is Ramadan, when there is no eating, drinking or smoking between sunrise and sunset. It usually occurs in October or at the beginning of November.

Gender issues

Islam regards men and women as equal, although it is discourteous to address Arab women except through their escorts. Some Arabs are still ill at ease with businesswomen, particularly obviously strong ones. Women are active in commerce, but they often employ men to handle their customer contact.

Business customs and taboos

Respect is given and expected; displays of impatience, arrogance and criticism, although possibly greeted impassively, may be considered insulting and will be held against the transgressor.

Arabs are generally tactile, considering a Westerner's reluctance to make body contact as cold and aloof. Shaking hands is mandatory; it is unfriendly to withdraw from a long grip, as it is held to establish friendship.

Prayers take place throughout every day and take absolute precedence.

Women in traditional dress should not be touched under any circumstances.

Business wardrobe

In general, men should wear long trousers and a long-sleeved shirt; women should wear modest and unrevealing clothes: skirts that are well below the knee; trousers are also acceptable; shirts with sleeves at least to the elbow. A skirt or trouser suit should be worn for formal meetings or with important people.

Welcome gifts

Craft gifts from home, flowers, confectionary and engraved gold pens are suitable. A high-quality compass may be appreciated as a symbolic gesture suggestive of finding the direction of Mecca – the Islamic holy city. Do not bring gifts or cards that show the human body; this is forbidden by Islam. Pictures of dogs or pigs are unwelcome, as they are considered unclean.

Food and drink
Arab food is generally spicy and pungent, and Arab cuisine is of the world's finest. Lunch is normally the biggest meal of the day. The consumption of pig meat is forbidden by the Koran – the sacred book of Islam.

Languages
Predominately Arabic.

Argentina

Business tips
Contact an *Enchufados* in your industry, a useful – if not essential – business intermediary with high-level commercial and government contacts. Personal relationships should be built before business proceeds. Executives often work long hours: appointments at 8.00 p.m. are not uncommon.

Formalities
Shake hands briefly with a brief bow of the head when introduced to men and women. Although most business people speak English, the reverse of your business cards should be in Spanish. Address people with their titles followed by their family names; for example, for engineers: *Ingeniero* Lopez; for lawyers: *Abogado* Lopez ... etc. People without titles should be addressed as *Señor* (Mr), *Señora* (Mrs); younger women should be addressed as *Señorita*. Hierarchies are very important; respect is offered to and expected by senior executives.

Gender issues
Women have been overtaking men in education and taking prominent roles in government and commerce. However, some older men find this difficult to accept. Women should initiate all handshakes with men.

Business customs and taboos

Decisions take longer than in Europe or the US, partly because of complex bureaucratic and legal structures. Appointments are necessary; casual drop-ins are not encouraged. Punctuality is expected of the foreign visitor but is not always reciprocated by the incumbents.

A firm, friendly handshake is important; it should be accompanied by a smile. Avoid discussing politics, particularly the Malvinas/Falklands.

Business wardrobe

Clothes should be modest. Dark suits and shirts are best for men and women; stylish ties for men. A high quality of cut and cloth is important and noted.

Welcome gifts

Scotch whisky and French champagne are suitable gifts, but not leather goods – they've got enough.

Food and drink

Tea or coffee is taken between 4.00 and 6.00 p.m., dinner from about 9.00 p.m. A great deal of beef is eaten and lots of domestic wine is enjoyed.

Languages

Castilian Spanish (with an Italian accent) is spoken by everyone; other languages include English, French, German and Italian, and a number of Indian languages.

Australia

Business tips

Australians are very approachable; they like straight talk, don't like being pressurised and hate being patronised. Business is conducted informally and is preferred without showmanship;

get to the point quickly. Do not suggest that the way things are done in your country is naturally superior.

Australians have a great ability to time-manage effectively: they divide their time between work and play really well.

Formalities
Business may be relaxed and casual, but dropping in unannounced isn't; appointments should be made even if you've dropped in from 5,000 miles away.

Don't be surprised to be called 'mate' by your colleagues, clients and waiters in restaurants. 'Mate' is a friendly way to address anyone. Women use it too. 'Sir' is an expression of respect, but first names are usually the mode of address from the moment you are introduced.

Gender issues
Women are becoming increasingly influential in business and government, but considerable chauvinism exists. Courtesies, such as opening doors for women, endure.

Business customs and taboos
Avoid criticism of nearly everything Australian, including how far it is from Europe. Don't agree with everyone; Australians respect people who stand up for their views. They distrust authority and snobbery. Behaviour is strictly informal – putting on airs leads to ridicule. You may be teased, but it's usually good-natured and requires a similar repost.

Discussions are generally direct and candid, but beware of crossing the line from irreverent humour into disrespect.

Business wardrobe
Conservative – suits in winter, trousers/skirts and shirts/blouses in summer. Businesswomen wear dresses and suits winter and summer. In less formal organisations, men wear smart 'walk shorts', knee socks, and shirts and ties.

Welcome gifts

Those with British backgrounds may appreciate good tea, marmalade, Scotch, shortbread biscuits, Jermyn Street shirts, etc. Asian and southern European business people will naturally enjoy gifts from their own countries.

Food and drink

Light lunches are taken and alcohol is not encouraged. Australians are proud of their wines, which are becoming world leaders.

Lamb and beef are popular, as well as southern Mediterranean and Asian dishes. Tea is taken from 4.00 p.m. and is often the main meal of the day. Business barbecues are sometimes the Australian equivalent of British cocktail parties.

Language

Predominantly English.

Belgium

Business tips

Language is not the only thing that separates Belgians; their codes of behaviour are equally different according to their regional identity. Bureaucracy is a proliferating art form in Brussels, and pristine documentation is appreciated. Most organisations belong to societies, fraternities and other trade institutes. Consider applying for appropriate memberships/ affiliations.

Punctuality is a must.

Formalities

Handshaking is mandatory when arriving and leaving; don't leave anyone out. Personal privacy is not to be breached; many Belgians prefer to separate their business from their home lives. English is accepted as the lingua franca.

Gender issues
Women hold some high positions in government and in some businesses, but they are still far outnumbered by men in senior executive positions.

Business customs and taboos
Rivalry exists between some Walloon and Flemish people, so check the ethnicity of your hosts before communicating. Some Walloons mock the Flemish characteristics and the jokes are reciprocated. Do not participate.

Although English is the business language, do not take this for granted, as it is not an official language.

Business wardrobe
Clothes are generally formal – suits, shirts and ties are a must in most businesses. Women wear suits, or jackets, skirts/trousers and shirts. Brussels and other big cities have large international communities whose outfits are smart, high quality and generally conservative.

Welcome gifts
Modest and useful branded items are suitable gifts.

Food and drink
Belgian cuisine and beers are acknowledged as among the world's best. Mussels, waffles, fries and desserts are all delicious.

Toasting is intrinsic to the dining ritual.

Language
There are three official languages within Belgium: Dutch (Flemish) is the official language in the north, French in the south and German along the eastern border.

People's Republic of China

Business tips

Punctuality is extremely important. Turning up late may be considered a personal affront. Decisions are usually taken by a number of committees and at the last moment. Be patient. Some partiality is shown to Communist Party members.

Take your own interpreter. Listening skills are very important. People often listen without visible responses. Do not interrupt your own seniors and certainly not theirs.

Formalities

Bow the head slightly when being introduced. Handshaking is acceptable.

Most activities are highly organised and rigidly regulated. The Chinese New Year, which varies according to the lunar calendar, is sacrosanct. Business is rarely conducted in the week preceding and following it.

Gender issues

Women have equal rights to men, but have yet to breach male bastions in most areas of politics and commerce.

Business customs and taboos

Don't mention Taiwan and don't criticise the Chinese leadership. If you aren't a party member, refrain from calling anyone 'Comrade'. Commercial concerns do not override the interests of the state and the Communist Party.

Colours are important throughout Chinese culture. Black and white is safest in business documents.

Business wardrobe

For men suits, shirts and ties that are conservative in cut and colour are appropriate. The same applies for women, but with high-necked blouses. Women should wear low heels. There is no need to pack a ball gown; for any occasion other than some diplomatic receptions, the outfit is as above.

Welcome gifts
In theory, gift giving is forbidden by law, but attitudes to this have loosened up. However, nothing of large monetary value should be offered. Suitable gifts include modern kitchen accessories, good foreign food and fine liqueurs.

Don't wrap gifts in black, white or blue (associated with funerals); red is favoured.

Food and drink
The country boasts a large number of different cuisines. Eat slowly and steadily at banquets; some are up to 20 courses. Don't leave an empty bowl, as it implies your host did not provide enough. Reach for serving dishes; they are not usually passed around the table. Toasting is an ongoing activity, started by the host. Businesswomen should avoid alcohol. If offered, take a sip and abandon it.

Languages
Three-quarters of the Chinese population speak standard Chinese derived from Mandarin. There are nearly 60 other languages or dialects. Fortunately, most Chinese business people speak English.

France

Business tips
With the exception of the tourist industry, France just about closes in August. Try to speak as much French as possible, to show your respect for the language; the French will consider it a compliment and will be happy to correct you. Know your business subject in detail as your hosts enjoy probing and debating at an intellectual level.

Formalities

Men often stand when a senior enters a room. Negotiations are conducted with formality and restraint. French business runs a constant battle against all-invasive and painstaking bureaucracy.

Shaking hands is customary when greeting and leaving. The touch may be light, but does not indicate the absence of an iron fist.

Print your business cards in French as well as English.

Gender issues

Address all women except young girls formally as *Madame*. Many French women still expect to be treated with traditional respect and courtesy. In business, a woman friend may be kissed three times on the cheeks. Some businessmen kiss male business friends in a brotherly way but usually stop at two. Do not assume that this is always the case, and certainly do not begin kissing people if you have only spoken to them on the telephone and you are meeting them for the first or second time.

Although women have made great progress, most top positions in business and government are held by male graduates of the exclusive *les grandes écoles,* a well-respected educational establishment.

Business customs and taboos

Professional titles are prized and prestigious. The French are sometimes conservative and reluctant to accept change. Administrative procedures may be considered more important than speed, flexibility and compromise. Organisations normally have rigid hierarchical structures, *and* you must be able to work at every level.

Business wardrobe

Great pride is taken in appearing chic, which means wearing good-quality, well-cut clothes, usually on the conservative side. French women use accessories with great skill. Famous labels are admired – particularly French ones.

Welcome gifts

Scotch whisky, stylish coffee-table books, cultural artefacts and executive toys without corporate branding are suitable gifts. Try to keep a gift personal. Business cards and company logos may be considered pushy so should not be in evidence on gifts or their wrappings.

Food and drink

Lunch is the accepted forum for business discussions – it can last for two hours. Drink frugally, if at all. The French take pride in their food, wine, coffee and liqueurs and enjoy accepting sincere compliments on their quality. Some courses that other national-ities would eat together are served separately in France, so don't nag the waiter if you think he's forgotten something.

Any observations or complaints must be addressed to your host, not directly to the restaurant management.

Languages

French has been the language of diplomacy for centuries and continues to fight hard against the relentless inroads of English.

Germany

Business tips

Decisions are usually made collectively and at several levels, and then implemented with vigour and attention to detail. Germans excel at long-term planning. They are not always comfortable with change, particularly when it is sudden or unannounced. Germans appreciate receiving information in great and pains-taking detail. Status is important, including your rank, the standing of your company, the size of your car and the quality and cut of your outfit.

Cut the jokes. Business is generally approached earnestly and solemnly. If possible, don't make appointments for Friday afternoons.

Formalities

Do not be overly friendly and effusive at first. Germans take time to warm up but when they do they can be affable and gregarious. Use the titles *Herr* or *Frau* along with a person's last name. *Fräuleine* is used for young girls.

Handshaking is expected all round – firm but brief, with eye contact. Titles are very important. Note them when exchanging business cards and use them at all times; for example, *Herr Professor, Herr Doktor.*

Gender issues

The tradition of *Kinder, Küche und Kirche* (children, cooking and church) as women's roles has not entirely disappeared. Women still have to fight harder than men to achieve senior positions. Men usually stand up when a woman enters a room.

Business customs and taboos

Germans like certainty and adhere to formal procedures. They are uncomfortable with vague statements and claims. Punctuality is essential. Jackets generally stay on in meetings.

Until a personal relationship has been established, conversation on personal issues should generally be kept to a minimum. Don't talk business during a meal; it's more acceptable before or after. Not all former 'East Germans' are comfortable discussing politics or life before the 1990 reunification.

Business wardrobe

Clothes should be conservative and conforming. Men and women managers mostly wear dark suits and white or light shirts. Smart jackets or blazers and trousers are alternatives in all but the most formal organisations. It's safest to follow the company style. Men's ties are generally quiet and subdued in colour and pattern.

Welcome gifts
Nothing extravagant. Small but good quality is the norm, and whisky, high-quality foodstuffs and teas are acceptable.

Food and drink
Sausages, veal and game are especially good in Germany. Salads are more often pickled than fresh. German white wines and beers are world class; pastries are huge and luscious.

Drinking moderately at business meals is acceptable. When toasting, look others briefly in the eyes.

Languages
German is spoken in a number of dialects and accents, usually according to historic regions. Other than German, English is commonly spoken in business and generally to a very high grammatical standard.

India

Business tips
Decisions are usually taken at the highest levels with middle managers as go-betweens. Close personal relationships are important, as is small talk and hospitality.

Communications – particularly by mail – can be slow, as is general bureaucracy. Use e-mail where possible. The word 'no' is considered abrupt; 'I'm not sure' is better. Be gently circumspect when disagreeing. People are not used to humour in business and may not understand puns and Western witticisms.

Visit between October and March to avoid extremes of climate. Check the packed religious calendars before making travel arrangements.

Formalities
Professional titles should be used, and unless you are close friends, Mr, Mrs and Miss. A strict hierarchy is customary in

many organisations, with deference to senior colleagues, whose opinions are rarely contradicted.

Handshaking is normal, but women should not initiate it with men. Greet people with the *Namaste* – place the palms together, bow the head and say '*Namaste*'.

Remove shoes before entering houses that have them lined up outside.

Gender issues

Outside modern cities and Westernised organisations, Hindus, Sikhs and Muslims avoid shaking hands with the opposite sex. If in doubt, use *Namaste* (*see above*). Men and women should not make physical contact in public other than handshaking.

Business customs and taboos

Titles are important: address people by them. Don't use a first name until invited to do so. An aggressive attitude may be perceived as a lack of respect. Do not point with the finger – Indian's do so with the chin.

Decisions are made from the top.

Business wardrobe

Suits and ties for men, with smart, short-sleeved shirts in summer. Women should wear smart conservative dresses or trouser suits, with upper arms, body, and legs well below the knee covered at all times. Wearing leather may be considered offensive by strict Hindus.

Welcome gifts

Chocolates and flowers are appreciated. Do not give leather goods to Hindus. Check that your host drinks alcohol (he won't if he is Muslim) and if so, bring good Scotch whisky and English gin.

Gifts should not be wrapped in black or white, which are thought of as representing misfortune.

Food and drink
Business lunches are preferred to dinners. Most Indians – other than those who are Westernised – are vegetarian and teetotal. Hindus do not eat beef – the cow is sacred; Muslims do not eat pork.

Eat with the right hand; the left hand is considered unclean.

Languages
Hindi is the official language, spoken by nearly a third of the population; English is used commercially and sometimes in official documents. Over 1,600 other languages or dialects are spoken. Major languages include Telugu, Bengali, Marathi, Tamil, Urdu and Gujarati.

Ireland

Business tips
Know what you want to achieve and be friendly. The Irish are great people to do business with.

Formalities
Be able to listen and talk – business and socially.

Gender issues
What are they?

Business customs and taboos
Relax, enjoy, work hard and play hard.

Business wardrobe
Very casual to extremely smart.

Welcome gifts
Yourself and your company.

Food and drink

Fresh organic produce, and pure black nectar with a creamy head (Guinness). Some of the best restaurants you'll ever visit are in Ireland.

Languages

Gaelic in many parts, but primarily English with some wonderful lilts.

Italy

Business tips

Most Italians prefer to conduct business in their own language – it's advisable to engage your own interpreter. Have your business card translated into Italian and include all your educational and professional qualifications. Status counts.

Elegance (*bella figura*) is appreciated, not just in dress but also in behaviour, in documents and in presentations. New ideas and concepts are invariably of interest – too much detail is not. The success of business proposals may be based as much on an Italian's gut reaction as on statistical back-up. As a matter of respect, Italians prefer to conduct business with the highest ranked executive possible.

Formalities

Seniority and age are highly and overtly respected. Business structures can be complex, but one thing is certain: hierarchy and the *cordata* (command structure) are extremely important. Older, established firms do not usually use first names between managers and staff. Wait until you are invited to use first names, otherwise stick to *Signor* or *Signora* plus the surname. Only young girls should be addressed as *Signorina*.

Gender issues

There are still very few women in senior management positions and comparatively few in the professions and government. Feminism has made few significant inroads. Women are generally treated with respect, but not as equals except in most families and in many family businesses.

Business customs and taboos

Honour and personal pride must be maintained. Beware of criticising companies, procedures, colleagues, Italy and Italians. The first meetings are usually held to assess you and your company. It will be to your advantage to project a warm and dignified demeanour. Structures can be rigid and strictly hierarchical so decisions can take time and deadlines can thus be missed.

Business wardrobe

Italy is a world leader in style; yours will be noticed. Business wear tends to be formal, but even when it is casual it is immaculate. Men wear well-cut dark suits in wool or silk, accessorised with stylish watches, cuff links, silk handkerchiefs and fashionable ties. Women wear simple, elegant and usually beautifully cut suits or skirts and shirts in subdued colours, with colourful accessories.

Welcome gifts

Small, unostentatious well-known brands of pens, calculators, key chains, etc. are suitable gifts, as are wallets and diaries – without company logos. When presenting flowers, it is traditional for there to be an uneven number. Don't use purple or black and gold paper as they have negative connotations.

Food and drink

Business is often conducted over lunch – which can run for three hours. Italian food is much more than pasta and pizza; there are at least seven different and generally excellent regional cuisines.

Italians are justly proud of their cheeses, wines, bread and sauces, among much else.

Sip the wine. Getting drunk is considered disgraceful.

Languages

There are several dialects of Italian. English is spoken by most international business people, but for a quick response, write letters in Italian.

Japan

Business tips

Unsolicited approaches are disliked. Get an introduction from a mutual contact such as a bank or other respected business associate. If a personal recommendation cannot be arranged, a letter of introduction is essential.

The first meeting is usually to get to know one another. Decisions are made by groups, and slowly. Bowing (and lowering the eyes) is the traditional greeting; your host may indicate how often and how low. Handshaking is a concession to the West; if it feels weak it is out of politeness and not lack of assertiveness.

Formalities

The basis of Japanese etiquette is respect – for individuals, age, companies, ideals, methodologies, etc. People prefer (and may insist on) conducting business with their exact equivalent levels from other companies. Conformity is part of the business culture, as is the vital importance of 'saving face'.

Business cards are essential; you should be seen to read them carefully. When one is handed to you, if it is given with two hands then you should receive it with two hands. Your business card should be printed in Japanese and English.

Management expressions should be translated into American (e.g. director = vice president) and then into Japanese.

Gender issues

Japanese businesswomen are becoming more powerful in business, particularly in the service industries. Japanese business people were once accustomed to dealing with women only in subservient roles. Some older people are still uncomfortable dealing with assertive women executives. Older Japanese women may be uncomfortable shaking hands with Westerners; don't move too close to them.

Business customs and taboos

Scant regard for Japanese rules of etiquette will seriously threaten a business relationship. Positions around a table are in decreasing order of importance. Behaviour is not as direct as in the West. The word 'no' (*iie*) is rarely used; 'maybe' is a more usual response. Do not pay compliments to individuals on good work. Compliments go to groups of people.

Business wardrobe

The Japanese for suit is 'Sebiro' derived from 'Savile Row', London. Dress should be conservative and neat, never casual. Lace-free shoes are useful, as you will find yourself removing them often as you enter homes and other places. Women should not wear high heels, to avoid towering over their hosts. Cotton clothes are essential in summer.

Welcome gifts

The ritual of handing over gifts is part of doing business. Single malt Scotch whisky, cognac, quality English tea, toys for hosts' children and high-status branded goods are suitable. They should be carefully wrapped (but not in black and white).

Food and drink

Traditional Japanese food includes rice, beans and raw fish. Allow your host to order for you initially. Sake (*Sakki*) – rice wine – is drunk warm.

Languages
Japanese. American–English is spoken in the corporate world.

Korea, South

Business tips
Koreans are persistent and patient, and they admire those qualities in others. Personal relationships are considered more important than business ones. Relationships may be difficult to establish with people who are not of your own age and rank. Make appointments and arrive on time even if your hosts don't.

A common gambit to put off making a decision is to say 'geul seh' – 'We will give it some thought'.

Formalities
Greetings should be made with a slight bow of the head and sometimes with a handshake, both while maintaining eye contact. Women don't shake hands.

Bow at the beginning of meetings. Bow for longer at the end of meetings. Exchanging business cards is very important. Leave theirs on the table in front of you for reference. The first name on a business card is the family name, then the given name. Address people by their title or by their title and family name.

Don't blow your nose in public: it is considered to be the height of rudeness, so just sniff.

Gender issues
Women have yet to achieve full equality; many are still expected to behave subserviently, but this is changing gradually. Inform your hosts in advance when a woman is in your party.

Business customs and taboos
Business can be done one-to-one with your contact reporting back to his company for final decisions. Maintain contact frequently as a matter of courtesy when you return home.

When your business group enters a room, ensure that it does so in order of rank. Do not drop formalities until and unless your hosts do.

Business wardrobe

Korean winters are cold and dry, summers hot and humid. Men should wear a conservative suit and tie and a white shirt; women should wear a conservative skirt and shirt/blouse or dress. People sit on floors in many restaurants so women should avoid short or tight skirts. Shoes are often removed when entering homes and some restaurants.

Welcome gifts

Good-quality tea and coffee, home crafts and branded company gifts are all suitable.

Food and drink

Rice and bean-based dishes are frequently eaten and the main meal is taken in the evening. Not much meat is eaten, but plenty of garlic is.

Language

Much of the Korean vocabulary is borrowed from Chinese characters. Korean is written in its own alphabetic form: *Hangul*.

The Netherlands

Business tips

The Dutch are consummate linguists, so it is usually unnecessary to translate your business cards into their language, but business and technical literature should be.

Being a direct people, they like to get down to business quickly after the introductions. They do not respond well to exaggeration and the unsubstantiated hard sell; solid back-up data is required. Direct language, including 'no', is preferred to procrastination. Consensus is valued in business. Many groups may be consulted before making decisions, so be patient. Once committed, they generally make fast progress.

Formalities

Punctuality is essential. Arriving without notice is not appreciated. Once made, appointments are changed under sufferance.

Shake hands when being introduced and state your name; it is not necessary to say, 'How do you do?' Professional titles are used; those without them should be addressed as *Meneer* (Mr) or *Mevrouw* (Mrs or Ms).

The Dutch prize and protect their privacy. Always knock and wait for permission before entering an office.

Gender issues

Women constitute around a third of the workforce and are quite rare in senior management. Males tend to treat women colleagues with traditional courtesy. Many women who leave to have families do not return to work.

Business customs and taboos

Whatever their rank, the Dutch do not assume superior attitudes; they react badly to any hint of being patronised. Letters are meticulously drafted and strictly formal, with all professional and academic qualifications applied. Promises of any kind are binding; break or 'adjust' even the smallest one and attitudes will harden and doors may be shown.

Business wardrobe

Styles vary wildly from formal dark suits and white shirts in financial services and traditional industries, to very relaxed jeans and sweaters in creative and some technological fields.

Jackets and trousers for men, and jackets and skirts or trousers for women are the most popular outfits. Designer outfits are rarely worn at work.

Welcome gifts

Good-quality, but unostentatious offerings such as whisky, pens, desk accessories and electronic gadgets are suitable gifts. Gift giving is regarded as a gesture of friendship, not business promotion. It is best to wait until a personal relationship has been established before offering a gift.

Food and drink

A working lunch is usually brief and modest, perhaps a sandwich or cheese and fruit. Snack breaks are taken in the morning and afternoon. Coffee is drunk profusely throughout the day, but tea is normal in the afternoon.

Dairy products are world class; so too are beer and gin.

Languages

Dutch is the official language. Some people also speak Frisian, Arabic or Turkish. In towns, most people speak excellent English.

Poland

Business tips

You are expected to be prompt. Poles vary in their adherence to timekeeping, but it's becoming tighter. Theirs is an extremely difficult language, so translating your literature and business cards into Polish and attempting a few words should generate goodwill. Many Poles speak very good English and the standard of education is extremely high. Poland boasts excellent commercial artists: your graphics must be very good to impress. Decision making in large enterprises is slow; smaller, younger enterprises are often much quicker at making decisions.

Formalities

Although this is a formal country that appreciates business and social rituals, new business leaders are often relatively young and more relaxed. When introduced, shake hands and use *Pan* (Mr) or *Pani* (Mrs) plus the family name. *Panna* (Miss) is for young girls. Women's hands are sometimes kissed.

Gender issues

Polish women are strong and often dominant in the home. Most women work, and some achieve high positions, particularly in academia. Women are usually accorded traditional courtesies, but behaviour that threatens male dominance can create discomfort. It is best to be subtle initially. Married women take their husband's last name; when the last letter is a vowel, it changes to an 'a'; for example Godebski becomes Godebska.

Business customs and taboos

Take plenty of business cards, and include your higher academic qualifications on them. Meetings often start at 8.00 a.m.; the working day ends at about 4.30 p.m. Most Poles respond badly to being on the wrong end of ultimatums or patronising behaviour. Avoid discussing politics, particularly in relation to Germany and Russia.

Business wardrobe

Traditional professions require suits for men and women in sober colours. Trousers and shirts or sweaters are acceptable in some new and small businesses.

Welcome gifts

Whisky, cognac, etc., but not vodka, make suitable gifts, as do good-quality tea and coffee, perfume and useful electronic devices.

Food and drink

Lunches are usually light and short. Business lunches often start in the late afternoon, after which people normally do not return to the workplace. Business dinners can go on very late.

Polish vodka is drunk heartily; wine is also consumed at business lunches. The most common toast is 'to your health'. Tea is usually drunk without milk and with lemon.

Language
Polish, an Indo-European language, is written in modified Latin alphabet.

Russia

Business tips
Be ready to write down your host's telephone numbers and details, as many small businesses do not print business cards. Try to locate the decision makers to avoid wasting time with powerless aides. Most businesses have rigid hierarchies, with decisions taken by the top person without reference to subordinates. In big organisations, it may be difficult to meet any useful people of middle level unless the general director has approved your initial approach.

Employ your own interpreter, and consider taking a Russian lawyer to interpret their complex commercial laws. Most Russians do not like compromises. They will stick to their guns with walkouts, threats and hot temper tantrums. Stay cool.

Formalities
Business cards should be translated into Russian (Cyrillic text) and presented Russian side up. A greeting can be a handshake with eye contact and stating your name.

Many meetings are minuted in the form of a *protocol*, which is agreed to and signed at the end. After a contract is signed, requests may be made to renegotiate certain terms; this some-times happens when the contract was not thoroughly read.

Gender issues
Women rarely occupy senior positions in business, although there are often female financial directors, chief accountants and

purchasing managers. Wives are often absent from business social events.

Business customs and taboos
Appointments should be confirmed several times as the date approaches. The visitor must be punctual, although the Russian host may not be. Flexibility is expected. Appointments often start late and go on longer than arranged. A Russian business maxim is: hope for the best, but prepare for the worst.

Business wardrobe
Wear conservative, good-quality and unostentatious clothes. If jewellery is worn it should be sparse. Dark suits and white shirts are favoured. Men's ties should be plain. Some men wear sweaters without ties. Women should wear skirts of modest length and preferably flat shoes.

Welcome gifts
All kinds of presents are welcome; they do not have to be wrapped. These include foodstuffs from home, whisky (not vodka, of which they've usually got plenty), and prestige brands of calculators, cameras, watches, cosmetics and toiletries, towels and cigarette lighters.

A dinner party is highly appreciated.

Food and drink
Business lunches and dinners are usually for celebrating a contract rather than for negotiating.

Allow your host to order, as menus are often full of unfulfilled promise. You are expected to drink, at least modestly – except if you have health or religious reasons not to – in order to help to establish close links.

Languages
Russian, an Indo-European language, is usually the only language spoken.

Singapore

Business tips

Singaporean executives are sophisticated and well travelled so book appointments well in advance. Despite their dynamism, negotiating in Singapore can require patience. Losing your temper or swearing in public is seriously frowned on. Personal relationships are frequently regarded as equally important as business-to-business ones. Singaporeans are generally quite forthright when negotiating but may tactfully try to avoid saying 'no', so look out for subtle hints of a negative response.

Formalities

Politeness is essential and valued. Introductions are generally made in order of seniority and handshaking is generally acceptable. There are many cultures and languages in Singapore, so ask your hosts, particularly senior people, how you should address them.

Much respect is accorded to exchanging business cards. Most Singaporeans present their cards with both hands, in which case the card should be received with both hands, and yours should be presented in the same way. When receiving a business card, study it carefully, and place it in front of you or in a front pocket; do not write on it or place it in your back pocket.

Gender issues

Men have traditionally dominated in most areas of business, but women are increasingly accepted and often hold powerful positions. Women's rights are protected under a women's charter.

Business customs and taboos

Take care to prevent any person from losing face, especially someone of authority. Executives tend to work far longer hours than their juniors.

Business wardrobe

It is always hot and humid, so dress may be casual and often without jackets. Bear in mind that office buildings, shopping malls, taxis, buses and the Mass Rapid Transit (MRT) in Singapore are all air-conditioned and therefore quite cool.

Businessmen wear dark trousers and a light-coloured, long- or short-sleeved shirt and a tie. Jackets may be worn initially. Businesswomen wear light-coloured, long-sleeved tops – plain or decorated – covering their upper arms, and a skirt or trousers. Singaporean women are quite attuned to the latest world fashions and adapt them for the workplace.

Some establishments, such as five-star hotels, may prohibit the wearing of round-necked T-shirts, or shorts and/or sandals in certain areas.

Welcome gifts

Strict anti-corruption laws restrict anything that may be considered bribery, particularly of officials, but token corporate gifts are acceptable. Gifts are normally given when a personal relationship has been established. Small, nicely wrapped craft gifts from home may be welcomed.

Food and drink

Business negotiations are usually kept to the workplace. Meals may be used to cement or celebrate a deal. Food includes everything from Malay, Indian and Chinese to pasta, sushi and McDonald's. Remember that Malays normally abide by Muslim dietary laws.

Language

The official languages are Malay, Chinese (Mandarin), Tamil and English. Malay is the national language and English is the language of administration. Most Singaporeans are bilingual, and speak English as well as a local language.

Spain

Business tips
It is crucial to select a Spanish representative to translate and act as your bridge to Spanish business customs and culture. Establishing a close and friendly relationship is a route to business success. The Spanish like high-quality business literature and respond well to polished product demonstrations.

Check frequently that your audience follows what you are saying in English. They may not admit difficulties, as that would be tantamount to losing face (*see* Formalities, *below*). Most Spaniards will listen carefully to arguments, but do not readily change their views, minds or decisions.

Formalities
Have business cards printed in Spanish on one side. People without titles should be addressed as *Señor* (Mr) or *Señora* (Mrs), and younger women as *Señorita*. Personal pride, dignity and honour are sacrosanct and must never be challenged.

Show your respect for Spanish customs and practices and emulate Spanish behaviour. Do not lose face yourself, or your credibility may be permanently damaged.

Gender issues
Few women currently reach senior management positions, although many are becoming politicians and judges. Although women may be treated with elaborate courtesy, the machismo culture survives.

Business customs and taboos
Business is generally hierarchical. In most companies, only the most senior person (*el padron*) makes decisions. Subordinates do the groundwork, although this is changing gradually.

First meetings are generally held to get acquainted; be open, friendly and dignified. Some companies close during *siesta* from

1.30 p.m. to 4.30 p.m., then work through until 7.00 p.m. or 8.00 p.m. Bedtime is relatively late so breakfast meetings don't usually start until 8.30 a.m.

Business wardrobe

High-quality, well-cut clothes reflect status. In traditional industries, men wear dark suits, white shirts and subdued ties. Women may dress less formally but with stylish elegance. Dresses and trouser suits are fine, particularly if they are of a high quality and designer branded.

Welcome gifts

Gifts are rarely given before the successful conclusion of a deal. They should not be extravagant and your company logo should not be prominent. Home crafts, good-quality pens, desk accessories and whisky are acceptable gifts and are usually opened on the spot.

Food and drink

Spanish cuisine is typically Mediterranean, replete with olive oil and garlic. Paella is a popular dish – made with saffron rice, seafood, sausage and vegetables. Lunch or an early evening meal may include *tapas* (counter-top hors d'oeuvres). Most Spaniards eat *tapas* with a drink and then eat late (from 9.00 p.m. onwards); they then talk or party until even later. Business lunches are common, but discussions are not usually held until coffee is served.

Languages

Spanish is the official language. The Basques, Catalans and Galicians have their own languages.

Sweden

Business tips

Presentations should include plenty of detail, case histories, systems and statistics, even ideology, but exclude emotion, the hard sell and humour. Compromise is normally not regarded as weakness. The Swedes are environmentally aware so include details on ecological impact wherever appropriate. Hands-on experience is valued; skilled workers are valued at least as much as managers.

Swedes are generally good listeners, big thinkers and logical persuaders; try not to interrupt them in mid-analysis.

Gender issues

Women hold a high status in business and government. There are equal numbers of men and women in the workplace, with equal pay. Nearly a quarter of managers are estimated to be women. Husbands and wives usually share domestic duties and costs.

Business customs and taboos

Decisions are generally slow to arrive but fast to be implemented due to the consensus decision process. Promptness is almost obsessive – including socially. When a business meeting is scheduled to finish at a particular time, it probably will do, even if matters are still arising. The same goes for start times. When promises are made they are generally delivered promptly.

Small talk is generally translated to mean 'dead talk'.

Titles are used before names (professor, doctor, engineer, etc.). First names are usually employed quite early in a relationship. Unless a close friendship has been established, personal issues and business matters are rarely mixed in conversation.

Business wardrobe

Stylish, high-quality, well-cut suits and jacket/trousers/shirts are worn. The Swedes are generally more informal and individualistic than most northern Europeans, especially outside the capital, Stockholm. Bright colours are acceptable in men's shirts and ties and women's dresses and shirts.

Welcome gifts
Alcohol is very expensive so good whisky, brandy, vintage wine, and so on go down well as gifts. Other suitable gifts include crafts from home, silk scarves and ties, and illustrated coffee-table books.

Food and drink
Smorgasbord is a favoured buffet-style lunch or dinner, with a large variety of hors d'oeuvres or main dishes of cold or hot savouries, including pâtés, smoked and marinated fish, meat-balls and smoked meats.

The customary toast is *skol* (cheers).

Language
Swedish is a Germanic language related to other Scandinavian tongues. The minority Lapps (Samis) have their own language. English and German are widely and well spoken.

Switzerland

Business tips
Be prompt for appointments. Always demonstrate soundness, seriousness and professionalism. The Swiss are cautious, not risk-takers; they respond well to quiet self-confidence but less well to the hard sell.

Formalities
Bring plenty of business cards. There is no need to translate the cards (into all four languages!) as most Swiss business people speak English, but check their preferred native language.

Wait to be introduced, then rise and shake hands. The Italian and French Swiss are generally less formal than the German Swiss. The Swiss are generally polite; they listen patiently and often take notes. Do not address people by their first names until invited to do so. For courtesy titles see sections on France, Italy and Germany.

Gender issues
Few women reach high positions in business or public life. They received the vote well after most 'civilised' countries. Four out of five employees in upper management are male.

The German word *Fräulein* and the French word *Mademoiselle* are no longer used except when addressing a young waitress. Women are generally addressed as *Frau* or *Madame*.

Business customs and taboos
Do not offer gifts of any kind until contracts are signed, as they may be perceived as attempted bribery (see Welcome Gifts, below). Avoid personal conversations unless a close friendship has been established.

Business wardrobe
Swiss men generally wear more colour than their British counterparts. In the German cantons, smart dress, that is suits, shirts and ties for men, is appropriate. In the French and Italian cantons, dress is less formal and slightly more flamboyant. Women wear suits with skirts or with well-cut trousers.

Welcome gifts
Quality cognac and champagne, coffee-table books and ethnic crafts are all suitable gifts, but see also Business Customs and Taboos, above.

Food and drink
Switzerland boasts superb ethnic-based cuisines, excellent cheeses and wonderful chocolate. Business breakfasts are rela-

tively rare, and business dinners often include spouses. Many offices close during lunchtime: between noon and 2.00 p.m. The Swiss generally enjoy drinking and they appreciate good food.

Language
German (Schweiz-Deutsch), French, Italian and Romansch (1 per cent).

United Kingdom

Business tips
If you are meeting people at a company for the first time and hoping to do business with them you will need to show that you know something about their company and product range, or the services they offer, to be taken seriously and to create a good first impression.

Pleasantries are usually exchanged before a meeting begins, even if the conversation is only about the weather or your journey to the meeting. As long as business people are knowledgeable about their product or service their age or rank will not deter a more senior person (customer) from listening to their sales presentation.

Formalities
A firm handshake, good eye contact and a positive greeting are expected when introducing yourself. Never introduce yourself as Mr, Mrs, Ms or Miss Lastname, as this is a courtesy form and should only be used by others when introducing you to another person. When introducing yourself, use only your first and last name.

You are expected to be punctual ... yes, even with the horrendous transport problems. If you are delayed, inform the person you are travelling to meet *before* you arrive late.

Gender issues

Women are generally respected in the workplace, as are men. The 'glass ceiling' phenomenon still exists for some women who work in male domains, although more and more women are being promoted to positions of authority. Few men now stand for a woman when she enters a room.

Business customs and taboos

Managers and sales people will very often be in a position to make decisions on behalf of their company, if they have been empowered to do so by their boss. Do not arrive expecting to see a person in a company without an appointment. Always confirm in writing any appointment, meeting or business details.

Business cards are essential. There is no standard format: they vary in colour, shape and content, some have qualifications shown whereas others do not, some people present them at the beginning of a meeting whereas others present them at the end. The only requirement is that they should be clean and not turning up at the edges.

Business wardrobe

This varies and is dependent upon the industry, but as a general rule a dark business suit and light or white shirt with an appropriate tie still appear to be the preferred form of business dress for men. Women wear smart skirt or trouser suits with toning or contrasting shirts.

Some companies, particularly in the IT sector, have very casual dress codes, and dress in media and design companies is smart–casual. A number of companies in the UK have 'dress-down' days where the employees wear smart–casual clothes as opposed to more formal business attire. If you are travelling to a planning or training meeting in the UK, it's always worth checking what the dress code is, as it does vary.

Welcome gifts

Gift giving and receiving tends to be limited to corporate gifts. Many organisations do not encourage gift-giving or entertaining of any kind because of the fear of being accused of corruptive practice.

Food and drink

A diversity of eating establishments can be found throughout the UK, from large fast-food chains to select restaurants; all tastes are catered for. The traditional and ever-popular British pub still offers a great pint of beer, and often good food, too.

United States of America

Business tips

Compared to most other commercial cultures, business is conducted at high speed (particularly in New York) with fast decision-making. Middle managers often have autonomy and can finalise medium-sized deals. Lawyers abound, nurturing a highly litigious business culture. Be cautious about what you promise. They are also widely used as advisors to avoid problems. You will negotiate most successfully if you do not appear too anxious.

Beware of time zones – there are four of them, plus two if you count Alaska and Hawaii. Don't forget the issue of distance; for example, it takes over four hours to fly from Washington DC to Los Angeles. An hour's flight from Los Angeles takes you only to San Jose – it won't even get you to San Francisco.

Formalities

When meeting, shake hands firmly, and make eye contact. Titles are not generally used. You'd never say 'Nice to meet you Vice-President X.' Informal first-name relationships blossom quickly but don't always develop.

Smoking is being stamped out in most business buildings, in some hotels and restaurants, and in most airlines. Small talk is short-lived at meetings; business is initiated briskly.

Gender issues
The US has led the world in gender equality; differences tend to be ignored in most businesses. Check if the local culture supports traditional behaviours such as deferring to women when entering rooms. If it's not done, it may be considered patronising.

Business customs and taboos
Punctuality is important, particularly in major cities – despite frequent traffic gridlock. Behaviour may appear casual but there's steely determination in most negotiations. Avoid remarks about race, religion, gender, age and physical attributes. Security is taken very seriously and it is expected that courtesy will be extended to everyone from airport security staff to air crew while they are fulfilling their functions.

Business wardrobe
This depends on where you work. Financial-sector people wear suits and ties; high tech is more casual; it is best to ask first. Americans are generally well groomed and well tailored, and they relish European couture.

Welcome gifts
Tax laws restrict the value of gifts to about $25, so there is not much of a gift culture in the US. Scotch whisky, high-quality English tea and traditional British foods like shortbreads go down well. If you are visiting an ex-pat, don't forget the Cadbury's chocolate.

Food and drink
Just about every cuisine in the world is represented in the US; New York is considered to have some of the best ethnic restaurants on Earth.

Business breakfasts are common. Business lunches may be short and sharp, and can be taken from 11.30 a.m. (Most people begin work between 7.30 a.m. and 8.00 a.m.). Table manners are different in the US, and many Americans cut their food, put down their knife and eat with their fork in the right hand. Business people don't often drink alcohol at lunchtime.

Languages
Spanish is rapidly catching up with English as the most-used language. Many other languages are spoken by the people of different cultures living in the US.

Further Reading

Philippa Davis, *Your Total Image, How to Communicate Success*, Piatkus, 1990

Dr Lillian Glass, *Confident Conversation*, Piatkus, 1991

Tom Jackson, *How to Find the Perfect Job*, Piatkus, 1993

—, *The Perfect CV*, Piatkus, 1991

Dorothy Leeds, *Powerspeak*, Piatkus, 1988

Allan Pease, *Body Language*, Sheldon Press, 1984

Derek Rowntree, *The Manager's Book of Checklists*, Corgi Books, 1988

Debrett's is the renowned name for addressing any social etiquette query. We used *Debrett's Correct Form*, edited by Patrick Montague-Smith, published by Headline, 2002, for the chapter on addressing dignitaries.

The list on page 24 has been adapted from *The Manager's Book of Checklists*.

Index

ABOUT LYNNE BRENNAN

Lynne Brennan runs Business Etiquette International, a successful company that provides personal development programmes and training in business etiquette. Her work includes coaching senior executives in business etiquette skills. For more information about Lynne Brennan's work, please visit her on
lynnebrennan@businessetiquetteint.com

To attend one of Lynne Brennan's stress-buster workshops in Ireland, contact Kevin Michaels at + 353 64 42785 for information.